Computer Monographs
GENERAL EDITOR: J. J. Florentine, Ph.D., Birbeck College, London

Computational Structures
An Introduction to non-numerical Computing

Computational Structures
An Introduction to
Non-numerical Computing

Patrick A. V. Hall

*Research Fellow, IBM United Kingdom Scientific Centre,
Peterlee, Co. Durham*

Macdonald and Jane's · London and
American Elsevier Inc. · New York

© Patrick A. V. Hall 1975

Sole distributors for the United States and Dependencies
and Canada:
American Elsevier Publishing Co. Inc.
52 Vanderbilt Avenue, New York, N.Y. 10017

Sole distributors for the Continent of Europe excluding the
British Isles and Commonwealth and the Republic of Ireland:
Elsevier Publishing Company
P.O. Box 211, Jan Van Galenstraat 335, Amsterdam, The Netherlands

Sole distributors for all remaining areas:
Macdonald and Jane's, Macdonald & Co. (Publishers) Ltd.
Paulton House, 8 Shepherdess Walk, London, N.1

Macdonald ISBN 0 356 08172 9
American Elsevier ISBN 0 444 19522 X
Library of Congress Catalog Card No. 74 17506

Text set in 10/12 pt. Monotype Times New Roman, printed by letter-
press, and bound in Great Britain at The Pitman Press, Bath

Preface

This book is intended to support a second course in computing, building upon knowledge which would have been acquired during an introductory course on programming. It would be the students first exposure to real computer science. The book introduces fundamental techniques of non-numerical computing, such as chaining, tables, and string-handling, which then lead on naturally to further courses on compiler construction, operating systems, data base management, artificial intelligence, and so on. The accent is on providing knowledge at all · levels, from abstract to machine, with methods which are transferable across a wide body of problems.

It is expected that the course would be backed up by courses on discrete mathematics, combinatorial statistics, as well as the obvious courses on programming and machine architecture.

The book starts, in the Introduction, by drawing the distinction between the concrete and the abstract structure inherent in the problem, and machine representations of that structure. Then in Chapter 1 abstract structures such as graphs and trees and stacks are surveyed, including also an account of recursion and the role of stacks within recursion. In Chapter 2 machine structure is discussed, introducing storage vectors and records before considering methods for inducing relationships within storage that are necessary for the representation of graphs and trees. A thorough discussion of methods of storage management for the dynamic allocation of storage to records and vectors within applications programs, is given. Finally control structures are discussed briefly and critically.

Chapters 1 and 2 introduce all the basic concepts and techniques, and the remainder of the book can largely be read in any order, applying these techniques to fundamental problems of computing. The order in which the chapters are given is thought by me to provide the easiest progression for the student.

Chapter 3 covers string handling. Applications are discussed before detailing methods for storing strings, managing collections of strings. Actual operations on strings are covered in two sections; string matches including various approximate matching methods and searches for substrings, and string manipulations for deletion and insertion of substrings, leading to a brief consideration of special methods for text editors.

Chapter 4 covers files and tables. Initially internal tables are very thoroughly considered, with techniques from sequential, to trees, to hashing. Algorithms are detailed, and evaluated for efficiency and area of potential applicability. Internal tables lead on to general consideration of external files, the constraints of sequential access and the need for batching, sorting, and the merge processing of files. The files in which more than one key is of interest are considered, giving a very brief introduction to data-base organisation and management.

Chapter 5 discusses sorting. It presents the best methods for internal sorting under four headings: selection, insertion, distribution, and merge. It considers also methods for sorting external sequential files. Special methods for discs are not considered.

Throughout the book the emphasis is on the analysis of the problem in the abstract, before considering computer solution of the problem. All too often during the development of computer science, machine-dependent factors have become entwined with the more abstract facets of the problem solutions, leading to very little carry-over from the solution of one computational problem to the solution of the next. A liberal use of diagrams has been exploited to clarify storage structures and the way these change during the execution of a program. At the end of each chapter there are a wide range of exercise problems: some of these are quite short, but some are sufficiently large to form programming projects to be performed during the course of a year.

Methods for a large variety of problems are given in detail: where these include details of method of storage, they will be called **routines**, otherwise **algorithms**. The method of presentation initially is as flowcharts (in Chapter 1), but thereafter is in an Algol-like notation, using **while** and **if** constructions with compound statements denoted by brackets [and]. Comments are made with the Algol-68 and PL/I device: anything contained between ¢s is a comment. I had originally intended to use publication Algol-60 throughout, but the necessary declarations, the need to use integers for pointers, lack of character handling, lack of a reasonable **while** control construction, and the need to be able to present methods at several levels of detail, persuaded me to adopt the informal notation that has been used.

Mathematical content has been kept small, so as not to bury the basic methods beneath a wealth of analytical detail. Only five theorems are formally stated, to establish important properties of tables and sorting, though other important properties are developed informally in the text. Complete analysis of algorithms, as exemplified by the books of Knuth, as well as formal proofs of the correctness of algorithms, are important, but not appropriate to a course in computing science of the level of this book. My mathematical notation has been kept 'standard', and is explained at its first use, though some conventions which occur often and might puzzle the unguided reader are the following: Pr(...) for the 'probability that . . .', and $\lceil x \rceil$ and $\lfloor x \rfloor$ respectively for the 'smallest integer greater than or equal to x' and 'greatest integer less than or equal to x'.

The content of this book has arisen from various courses on non-numerical computing that I have given at the City University. Around thirty hours of lectures would be appropriate for such a course, though I often had to cover the material in half that! I have found that the idea of chaining is very readily appreciated, but that the programming of problems involving chaining does gives the majority of students considerable difficulty: only practice will get round this and when giving courses the most successful formula that I have found is to pose the problem at the beginning, work through the solution introducing the new techniques that they will need, before launching into the course material. Modularising the problem and requesting the solution in phases, with tight schedules (as in Exercise 3.4.5) proved very successful, whereas exercises run with very little problem analysis and no deadlines proved less successful for the majority of students, but did allow the brilliant student to show his worth.

A bibliography has been included, to indicate where reading material can be found should any reader wish to pursue a particular subject further. The bibliography is not intended to acknowledge the literature sources which have contributed to this book—the list would be too vast, and would not be appropriate to this form of book.

I wish to thank the many students who have attended my courses on non-numerical computing and computational structures—I hope that they learnt as much as I did. I must also thank the many colleagues with whom I have discussed problems in non-numerical computing (notably Andrew Holt at City University and Stephen Todd at IBM), and who have either directly or indirectly contributed to my knowledge and understanding, and hence to this book. I also thank Geoff Dowling, who read an earlier version of this book, and made suggestions which (we both hope) have led to a more understandable text. Finally, I thank Tina Hall, who has encouraged and supported me during the writing of this book.

Patrick A. V. Hall
8 August 1974

Contents

Introduction

In this book we are going to study in depth various computing methods which are basic to most non-numerical (and indeed, numerical) uses of computers. The techniques include chaining, tables and file handling, plexes, and so on, techniques which recur again and again in systems programming, on-line computing, graphics, information retrieval, etc. Throughout the book we shall draw heavily on examples and case-studies to motivate the techniques.

However, to satisfactorily solve a problem using a computer one must be able to consider and analyse the problem in the abstract, before attempting to apply our tool, the computer, to the solution of the problem. Accordingly, we shall have frequent recourse to simple mathematical notions such as graphs and trees. These are introduced in the first chapter, though some prior experience of discrete mathematics and the modern mathematical notation would greatly assist the reader.

In developing computer-based methods, it will be assumed that the reader has some familiarity with both high-level and machine-level use of the computer, though no specific machine or language will be necessary for the understanding of the text. Where the computer methods are given in detail, a combination of diagrams and flowcharts will be resorted to. Most often the 'flowcharts' will take the form of a numbered sequence of steps, using a notation to detail the steps rather like Algol-60: this form of 'flowchart' has been used so that the method can fit into the flow of the text, rather than having to appear in a separate figure, and to make the methods easier to appreciate through their presentation by 'structured programming' techniques.

What is computation? Certainly numerical calculations must be classed as computation, but so also must many other activities that do not yield numerical results. Using and maintaining a file in an office, playing chess, finding your way from one part of a town to another part of the town, must also all be classed as computation if we are not to take too narrow a view of computing. We shall say

$$\text{COMPUTATION} \equiv \text{MANIPULATION OF DATA}$$

where data is any information recorded about our problem. Data can be viewed as composed of a collection of **units** (this collection is often called the **data-base**), these units being interrelated in some way. These relationships are the **structure** of the data, and it is this structure that we must exploit in the solution of our problem.

We humans, in going about our business in the world outside, continuously and quite unconsciously exploit the structure of the physical world, its regularities, to save ourselves effort. And that is what we must do if we use a computer.

In solving our problem we may wish to impose further structure on our data, or subsets of the data. That is legitimate providing that we don't thereby violate other structure that is inherent in the data.

The data in our problem is the **static** component of our problem. When we actually actively manipulate the data, a second **dynamic** component enters (this dynamic aspect is commonly made static through the use of flowcharts!) and this dynamic component also has a structure. This dynamic part is the **algorithm** or sequence of steps with which our problem is solved: note that an algorithm actually prescribes many possible computations, one of which is actually 'executed' as a function of the data.

So far we have been discussing our problem in the abstract. If we propose a method of solution in the form of an algorithm, this would also be abstract, being expressed perhaps with the use of pencil and paper and some agreed notation, but nothing more.

When we come to the actual execution of a computation employing some abstract algorithm, and using physical machinery, we encounter further problems. The machinery might be very simple, such as a card index in a library, or very sophisticated like a digital computer. Whatever it is, it has an inherent structure, just as a motor-car has a structure, being composed of an engine, body, wheels, etc., these in turn being interconnected, and composed of smaller parts, nuts and bolts, and so on. This inherent structure imposes limitations on the machinery and the way in which it can be used. A motor-car cannot fly, but a helicopter can. Algorithms which work well with one kind of computing machinery, may work inefficiently or even not at all on other machinery. Thus we shall have to examine the structure of the machines, digital computers, that we shall use. We shall look at both low-level (assembly code) and high-level structures of the computer, and critically consider how well the structures there match up with requirements of algorithms we commonly wish to employ. Within the computer, we shall find two aspects of structure, static and dynamic, associated with respectively the storage and the control of the computer.

We have now examined computation in its various aspects, and found two levels at which a computational problem can be examined, the abstract and the concrete. At both these levels there are two facets, the static and the dynamic. In all these the primary concern is with structure. We shall call all forms of structure collectively, COMPUTATIONAL STRUCTURE, and then call the abstract static component associated with the problem data, the INFOR-MATION STRUCTURE, the abstract dynamic component the ALGORITHM STRUCTURE, the concrete static component the STORAGE STRUCTURE, and the concrete dynamic component the CONTROL STRUCTURE. I have deliberately avoided the term 'data-structure' since this is so often used in the literature in an ambiguous way. The distinctions made above are of vital importance if we are to embark upon the computational process with any hope of rationality. There is a good case for a further distinction on the static side between information structure, **access paths**, and storage structure, which becomes especially important with multi-level storage using discs. We will, of course, consider access paths, but only as part of the process of translating from the abstract information structure to the concrete storage structure.

In this book our concern then is the translation or realisation of abstract structures, both informational and algorithmic, within the concrete digital computer. The actual creation of algorithms will not be directly tackled, though it is hoped that the approach to problem specification and final solution taken in this book will help those who find the production of algorithms difficult. The book by Dahl, Dijkstra, and Hoare on structured programming is recommended to anyone who wishes to know more about a systematic approach to the writing of programs and the generation of algorithms.

1 Abstract information and algorithm structures

We shall now survey the mathematical structures that are most important in computational problems. This survey is not intended to be comprehensive, but rather to focus the readers' attention upon structures, or aspects of structures, which he may otherwise have glossed over, or missed altogether.

1.1 Some important notation

The building blocks of mathematical theory are **sets**, which we shall always denote by capital letters. Sets contain elements, which we shall always denote by small letters, using the symbol $\in$ to denote set membership. Thus $x \in X$ means x is an element, a member, of set X. We can also write a set by listing its members, enclosing them in braces, thus $\{x, a, y\}$.

The number of elements in a set X is called its **cardinality** and is written $|X|$.

If we have two sets X and Y, we can consider pairs of elements, the first of which is drawn from X and the second of which is drawn from Y. We call this the **Cartesian Product** of X and Y writing this as $X \times Y$. Thus

$$X \times Y = \{(x, y) \text{ such that } x \in X \text{ and } y \in Y\}.$$

A **relation** between X and Y is any subset of $X \times Y$. A special kind of relation is called a **function**; this has the extra restriction that any y in set Y is related to at most one x in X. If f is a function (then $f \subseteq X \times Y$) relating X and Y, we write $f : X \to Y$, and $y = f(x)$ to denote the element of Y to which x is related. Relations of various kinds are used continuously in the modelling of structure in computational problems.

For some special sets, we shall use symbols with special meaning, notably R for the real numbers, and Z for the integers.

1

1.2 Indexing and ordering

An **indexing** on a set X is a function or mapping I, where $I:X \to \{1,2,3,...,|X|\}$. One can have more general indexings, but we will mostly use the term in the sense above.

Indexings can enter our problems in essentially two ways: they give us means of refering to individual elements by number. We would either want to step through the elements as in adding a set of numbers together, or we would want to jump around the set inspecting the elements in some unpredictable order. Indexings are usually introduced for notational convenience, and where this is done, we must clearly recognise the fact. We shall see an example later in graphs where this happens. If we have an indexing on a set, the temptation is to store the data set within the computer as an array: we shall see later that this is often very unwise.

A **total ordering** on a set X is a relation '$\leq$' $\subseteq X \times X$ in which $x \leq x$ (or more correctly, $(x,x) \in \leq$), for all x and y, either $x \leq y$, or $y \leq x$, but not both unless $x = y$, and in which $x \leq y$ and $y \leq z$ implies $x \leq z$.

Orderings are familiar with numbers, but also exist for words in a language (a dictionary is an ordered set of words), and for other objects. Orderings will come into computing for use primarily in the context of sorting; in sorting, we are given an indexed set, and want to change the indexing so that $x_i \leq x_j$ if and only if $i \leq j$. (*Note.* We are writing x_i to mean that element of X whose index is i.)

In some problems, **partial orderings** arise. This is like a total ordering, but without the second of the requirements, that all pairs of elements be related. For example, books in a library are partially ordered by content: we can say one book is less than another if the subject matter that it covers is a subset of the subject matter covered by the second book. This structural property relating books can be used to advantage in automatically retrieving information from a library.

1.3 Strings

A string is a sequence of symbols drawn from a finite set or alphabet. For example, if A is the set $\{0, 1\}$, then 0011110010100 is a string over A. If the alphabet that we are considering consists of all letters, numerals, punctuation symbols used within this book, then this book could be considered as a string.

Often in computing we are dealing with strings of symbols some of which we interpret as numbers, others as names, etc. Special symbols might be used to separate one string from the next, or a change of alphabet might do this. Often we think of the string as being a sentence in some language.

Important properties of strings are:

(i) They are of variable length, although the alphabet is fixed.

(ii) We usually access the symbols in sequence from one end, when the ordering aspect of the sequence and not the indexing is important.

(iii) If the string is thought of as being a sentence in some language, this means that there are constraints about which symbols can occur together. That is, we have more structure. This structure is commonly expressed in the form of a syntax or grammar. The reader who wishes to know more about the structure of languages is recommended either the books on compiling by Gries, and by Hopgood, or the theoretical book by Hopcroft and Ullman.

In processing strings, typically we want to search the string for the occurrence of a particular symbol or symbol group, and mark it, substitute for it, or perform some other action as part of an editing operation, or linguistic analysis.

1.4 Graphs

A graph is relation of set with itself, in which extra properties can occur. There are several varieties of graph, all of which have significance within some problem or problems.

A **directed graph** is the system $G = (X,U)$, where X is a set of elements called **nodes** or **points,** and U is a relation on X (that is, $U \subseteq X \times X$) called the **edges** or **arcs** or **lines** of the graph. If a and b are nodes, and (a,b) is an edge, we say that the edge goes from a to b.

An **undirected graph** is a graph in which direction of the edges is removed: the simplest way of characterising this is to say that

3

$(a,b) \in U$ if and only if $(b,a) \in U$. A graph can be **weighted** if additionally we are given a function $w: U \rightarrow R$. This specifies the **weight** or **length** of each edge in the graph. Usually all the weights would be positive.

A road-map in which the towns are nodes and the roads the edges serves as a good example of a weighted graph. The graph would be directed if any of the roads were one-way only.

A graph may further have either its nodes or its edges (or both) **labelled**—that is, we would have a mapping from X or U or both to some labelling set. This labelling set could be a set of numbers, or a set of strings. A road-map would normally have labelled nodes (labelled with strings, the town-names).

Object	Typical problem	Nodes	Edges	Weights	Labels	
					Nodes	Edges
Road-map	Find shortest route	Towns	Roads (directed)	Distance	Name	Route name
Game of chess	Select best move	Board position	Legal move (directed)	Time taken	Position	Who moved
15-puzzle game	Select sequence of moves	Board position	Legal move (undir.)	—	Position	—
Program flowchart	Execute program, analyse efficiency	Box	Transfer of control (directed)	—	Actions	Yes/No conditions
Social system	Divide into social groups	Individual people	Know each other (directed)	Strength of bond	Name	Type of bond
Line drawing of straight lines	Compare two pictures	Line junctions and ends	Lines (undir.)	Length	Position (x, y)	—
Dictionary	Check if two words similar	Words	Cross-references	—	Word	—
Electrical circuit	Find all currents voltages	Junctions	Components	Impedance	Voltage	Type of component
Chemical molecule	Search for sub-structure	Atom	Bond	Strength	Name of atom	Type of bond

Table 1.1 *Some everyday examples of graphs*

Other examples of graphs (see Table 1.1) are line drawings, where nodes are the points of intersection of the lines, and are labelled by 2D vectors indicating the position of the node on the surface on which the drawing exists; electrical circuits, in which the junctions of the components constitute the nodes, with the edges being the electrical components suitably labelled to indicate the type and value of the component; a social system in which the individual members of the society are the nodes, and the edges are the social ties of kinship, friendship, debt, etc.

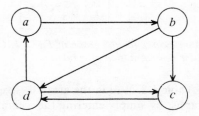

Fig. 1.1. Pictorial representation of a graph. Graph G = ({a, b, c, d}, {(a, b), (b, c), (c, d), (d, a), (b, d), (d, c)})

Typical problems could involve comparing graphs (say line drawings in picture recognition), extracting a shortest route through a road-map, finding a set of simultaneous equations from an electrical circuit, or finding a critical edge in a graph whose removal would lead to the breaking up of the graph into two distinct and separate regions.

We can represent a graph, a particular graph, in many different but equivalent ways. The definition provides one way, and let us consider the alternatives through the medium of an example: $G = (X,U)$, where $X = \{a,b,c,d\}$ and $U = \{(a,b),(b,c),(c,d),(d,a),(b,d),(d,c)\}$. Note that we have used symbols to differentiate between the nodes, but that these symbols are in no way node labels. However, we shall treat them as such so that the relationship between this and other representations is clear. The first alternative is to use a picture: this is shown in Fig. 1.1. We shall use such pictures frequently, since they give an immediate appreciation of the structure. The second alternative is to use an array, indexing the nodes in some arbitrary manner, and setting the (i,j) entry in the array to 1 if there is an edge from the ith node to the jth node, setting it to 0 otherwise.

5

TO

	a	b	c	d
a	0	1	0	0
b	0	0	1	1
c	0	0	0	1
d	1	0	1	0

FROM

Table 1.2. Connection matrix for the graph of Fig. 1.1. Compare this with the usual tabular representation of a relation.

This is shown in Table 1.2. Within the array it is very easy to represent weighted graphs, by simply entering the weight as appropriate, and adopting some convention for the absence of an edge. This matrix is called the **connection matrix** and plays a significant role in the theory of graphs. It also suggests one means of storing graphs in the computer, but, as we shall see, this is not the only means. The third alternative is to view the edges as a mapping, $U:X \rightarrow 2^X$ where 2^X means the power set of X, the set of all subsets of X. For the example, this edge mapping is shown in Table 1.3. If there is more

$x \in X$	$U(x) \subseteq X$
a	{b}
b	{c,d}
c	{d}
d	{a,c}

Table 1.3. Incidence matrix or operator representation of the graph of Fig. 1.1.

structure in the problem, the mapping can be summarised by formulae or other computational prescriptions. In the example, if we equate $a = 1$, $b = 2$, $c = 3$, and $d = 4$, we can partially summarise the edge mapping by $U(i) \equiv i+1 \; MOD(4)$. This representation sometimes is called an 'operator representation', and is important in automatic problem solving and game playing, where the underlying graphs are not stored explicitly in the computer, but implicitly as a set of rules for going from one node to the next. If we were to draw Table 1.3 differently, it would look like a matrix in which the rows were for nodes, and the columns for edges: this matrix is called the **incidence matrix** of the graph; this should become clearer through a second example in which the edges have been labelled in some uniform manner, as in Fig. 1.2 and Table 1.4.

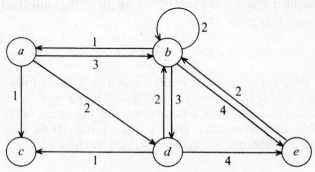

Fig. 1.2. A graph with labelled edges.

EDGE

	1	2	3	4
a	c	d	b	
b	a	b	d	e
c				
d	c	b		e
e		b		

NODE

Table 1.4. Incidence matrix representation of the graph of Fig. 1.2.

A graph is **regular** if each node has the same number of edges leaving each node, and the same number of edges entering each node. In representing graphs within the computer, regularity will be exploited where possible, and we shall see many examples in due course.

A **path** through a graph is a sequence of nodes $\{x_1, x_2, ..., x_m\}$ such that $\{(x_1, x_2), (x_2, x_3), ...\}$ are edges. Two nodes are **connected** in the graph if there is a path leading from one to the other. A graph is **weakly connected** if, viewed as undirected, all pairs of points are connected, while it is **strongly connected** if all pairs of points are connected when direction is taken into account. The **length** of a path in a weighted graph is the sum of the length of the individual edges comprising that path. Thus

$$w(\{x_1, x_2, ..., x_m\}) = \sum_{i=1}^{m-1} w(x_i, x_{i+1})$$

We shall say a graph is **empty** or **null** if it has no **nodes** (and therefore no edges), and denote this special graph by $\emptyset$.

The study of graphs is a fascinating and important study in its own right, and the reader is urged to read further. There are numerous texts available, for example that written by Harary.

1.5 Trees

We now consider a special kind of graph: a **tree**. We shall see various kinds of tree. A **free tree** is an undirected graph which

 (i) has no cycles (i.e. loops or closed paths), and
(ii) is connected.

Fig. 1.3(*a*) shows a free tree. If we only insist on property (i), and allow the free tree to consist of several different parts, we obtain a **forest** as in Fig. 1.3(*b*).

Now very often we shall single out a particular node for special attention, calling this node the **root**, in which case the tree becomes a **rooted tree,** or **oriented tree,** or simply **tree** since this is the variety of tree that we most often use.

We shall indicate the root on diagrams by an arrow, as in Fig. 1.3(*c*), or the root will be obvious from the orientation of the diagram, with the root being the **topmost** node. (This may appear somewhat bizarre to those who think of biological trees, but the drawing of trees in computing with the root at the top is now a firmly established convention. In thinking computationally about trees, one starts at the root, and placing the start at the top agrees with usual conventions concerning books and diagrams.)

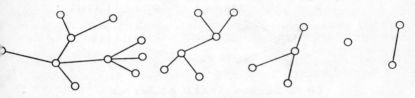

(*a*) *A free tree.*   (*b*) *A forest of four free trees.*

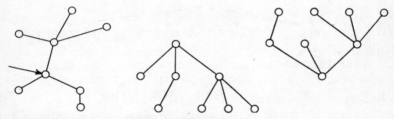

(*c*) *Rooted trees: all three trees are equivalent.*
(*c1*) *Root indicated*   (*c2*) *Root at top.*   (*c3*) *Root at bottom.*
      by an arrow.

Fig. 1.3. Graphs which are trees or forests.

Now a rooted tree has a natural direction defined within it, namely away from the root, and towards the root, and thus it is both natural and common to define trees as directed graphs in which the directions are all either away from, or all towards, the root. Thus we could define a rooted tree as a directed graph in which:

  (i) There is a unique special node called the root which has no edges leading into it.
 (ii) All other nodes have exactly 1 edge leading into them, and an arbitrary number of edges leading out of them.
(iii) There are no cycles (or equivalently, the graph is connected).

9

In this definition we could reverse the directions of the edges to obtain an equally acceptable definition. Very often the direction in the tree is a natural part of the structure of the real-world object that we are modelling using trees. Fig. 1.4(a) and (b) show two family

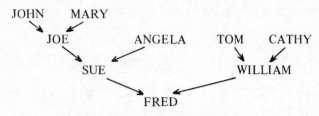

(a) *The ancestors of FRED, a binary tree.*

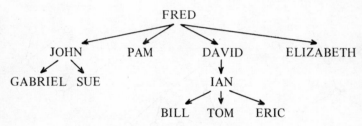

(b) *The descendants of FRED.*

Fig. 1.4. Two family trees.

trees in which the directions of the arrows in the tree are the 'arrows of time', with direction going from parent to offspring. One very often in trees talks of parent nodes, and sons and daughters of nodes (this is mixing our metaphors somewhat). Note that intermarriages of people with a common ancestor leads to convergence within the tree, so strictly speaking a family tree is not a tree!

The name 'tree' has arisen for obvious reasons, and the analogy is commonly extended to further terminology. Thus edges are **branches**, and the nodes at the extremities of the branches are the **leaves**. In computing, trees don't remain fixed: they grow, and nodes earlier thought of as leaves turn out to be buds which sprout, and even sometimes wither!

Let us now consider yet another way of defining a tree, this time recursively, defining trees in a way which allows one to build trees out of smaller trees (or subtrees):

(i) A set $\{n\}$ consisting of a single point or node n, is a tree, as below, with its single node being both root and leaf.

$$\textcircled{n}$$

(ii) Given a node n and trees $T_1, T_2,..., T_m$ we can form a new tree

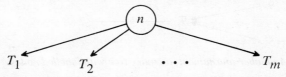

where n is the root, with edges leading to (or from, or to-and-from) the roots of the subtrees, $T_1,..., T_m$.

This way of looking at trees as composed of smaller trees is important, and often exploited in solving problems connected with trees. We say that trees are recursive structures. Later in this section we will see an example where this recursive structure is exploited, and later in the text we will see many more examples.

Trees occur frequently in everyday life, and are well known in the form of family trees (Fig. 1.4), and hierarchical organisation structures. Without a doubt, the tree is the most important structure within computing. A few examples follow, and throughout this book we come back again and again to trees. We will see that very often we treat the edges leaving a node in a definite order, talking of the left-most edge, and so on. Sometimes this order is only for convenience of communication, but sometimes it is an important part of the structure of the problem.

In sorting numbers, a common strategy is to impose a tree structure on the problem. We shall see several forms of this, the simplest being tournament sort—the numbers are arranged into a tournament, and are paired off and played off with the largest number gaining promotion to the second round where the winners are again played off in pairs, and so on until the largest emerges as winner, and is placed in the correct position in a new sequence of numbers. Fig. 1.5 shows an example of such a tournament. With the winner removed, the tournament can now be replayed to select the second

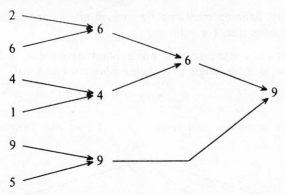

Fig. 1.5. A number tournament, a binary tree with labelled nodes.

best, and so on. Repeating this process allows us to eventually have selected all the numbers in descending order, enabling us to thus sort the numbers. This is the basis of some efficient methods for sorting numbers which we study in depth later. The binary tree, not inherent in the data, assists the sorting.

Consider Fig. 1.6. This shows a tree **traversal**: by following the

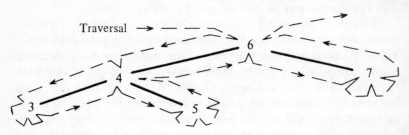

Fig. 1.6. A tree traversal. Showing the three points at which a node is encountered.

broken line in the direction of the arrows we traverse or walk round the tree, starting at the root and ending up at the root. On the way round we pass a node in general three times, and we pass every node at least once. In traversing the tree we can systematically do something to every node of the tree—for example let us print out the node labels. If we print out the node labels only at the first encounter, we obtain the sequence 6,4,3,5,7, while if we print them at the second encounter we obtain 3,4,5,6,7, and at the third encounter we obtain

12

3,5,4,7,6. These three traversals are known respectively as **pre-order**, **in-order**, and **end-order** (or **post-order**) traversals, and are detailed below.

ALGORITHM 1.1. *Pre-order binary tree traversal*
If the tree is empty then exit.
Otherwise process the root, and then traverse the left subtree, and then traverse the right subtree, and finally exit.

ALGORITHM 1.2. *In-order tree traversal*
If the tree is empty, then exit.
Otherwise traverse the left subtree, then process the root, and then traverse the right subtree, and finally exit.

ALGORITHM 1.3. *End-order tree traversal*
If the tree is empty, then exit.
Otherwise traverse the left subtree, traverse the right subtree, and then process the root, and finally exit.

We shall make great use of the in-order traversal in tables and sorting. The other traversals are important in other applications, such as language analysis, which we will not study here.

We will see trees in many contexts other than those above, but these examples should suffice.

We shall require, and use often, a very special degenerate kind of tree, called a **linear tree**, which only has at most one edge leaving or entering any node, as is illustrated in Fig. 1.7. Clearly a total ordering

Fig. 1.7. A linear tree, labelled as a string 'text'

on a finite set defines implicitly a linear tree, and strings have the structure of a linear tree.

There is an important structure midway between a graph and a tree. This is the **lattice**, a **directed** graph that is connected and has no cycles (compare this with the definition of a tree, given at the beginning of this section). We can think of lattices as directed trees in which we have allowed some convergence of paths, more than one edge entering a node. Hierarchical structures with common substructures are lattices, and so are family trees where intermarriages have occurred. Commonly lattices are defined in a slightly more restricted form than this, having a single 'root' and a single 'leaf', the common mathematical example being the set of all subsets of a given set, with set inclusion defining the directed edges. Fig. 1.8

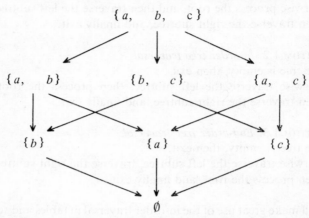

Fig. 1.8. A lattice of the subsets of set (a, b, c). The directed edges show set inclusion.

shows the lattice for a set of three elements. Lattices in mathematics are treated as special partial orderings, and not as graphs.

1.6 Stacks and queues

Stacks and queues are dynamic structures, providing for the addition to or deletion from a set of elements. Queues will be familiar, all too familiar, from everyday experience. Stacks are also familiar in the form of piles of plates or trays in a refectory. In a queue the element that entered first, leaves first, while in a stack the element that entered last leaves first.

It is stacks that we are primarily interested in, so let us define the idea more closely. A stack consists of a linear tree together with three functions or operations: POP, PUSH, and TOP, which have the following effects:

POP, erases the root of the stack linear tree.

PUSH(*a*), forms a node with value *a*, making this the root of the extended tree, with an edge leading to the previous root.

TOP, produces as result, the value of the root of the stack tree.

State one: TOP = x

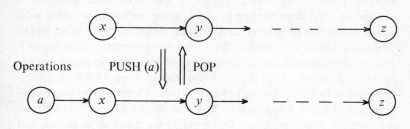

Operations   PUSH (a) POP

State two: TOP = a

Fig. 1.9. The operations on a stack.

These operations are illustrated through diagrams in Fig. 1.9. We see that PUSH(**a**); $V \leftarrow$ TOP; gives us the value **a** for variable V, while sequence PUSH(**a**); POP; has no net effect.

Stacks are known by several other names: nesting stores, push-down stores, and last-in-first-out (LIFO) stores. For us their primary use will be in parameter tracking in recursive algorithms, which we will see in the next section, though they also occur in other contexts such as subroutine linkage, priority interrupts, the shunting algorithm, where the function of the stack, though somewhat obscured, is essentially that of parameter tracking. Sometimes stacks have extra operations for accessing elements away from the root.

.7 The structure of algorithms

We now have the tools to analyse the dynamic aspects of an abstract computational problem. The dynamic aspect, the part that incorporates the changes with time, is the algorithm, and traditionally

15

these have been displayed using flowcharts, or some equivalent method (ignore algorithmic languages such as Algol-60). Flowcharts are directed graphs in which the nodes are labelled by specific primitive actions to be performed. However in algorithms there is a very important hierarchical structure which is lost in flowcharts. Problems consist of subproblems each of which have their own particular method of solution. This hierarchical structure continues to many levels, with subproblems being very possibly common to different parts of the over-all problem. The hierarchical structure is not lost in good flowcharting practice, using outline flowcharts, with boxes expanded to greater and greater detail, and no more detail contained within one subflowchart than can be immediately appreciated, without flowcharts continuing on second or more pages (except by box expansion). Alas, this is all too seldom done. This hierarchical structure is tree-like, but not strictly a tree. There will be some convergence of paths from root to leaf, due to the sharing of common subproblem subalgorithms. Technically this gives us a lattice, but the distinction is not important, for conceptually we could duplicate subalgorithms and avoid convergence.

Thus an algorithm is a graph which is itself highly structured in the form of a tree. In the creation of algorithms it is the hierarchical decomposition which is important, and in the appreciation of other peoples algorithms, the hierarchical structure also plays a vital role. Thus in the expression of an algorithm the hierarchical structure must be preserved and made explicit.

In many problems, such as mnemonic decoding, portions of an algorithm can become very confused if represented by a flowchart. The flowchart becomes heavily branched. Now a flowchart is but one representation of the graph which is the algorithm, and we are free to use other representations. The heavy branching is typically associated with tests, switches, or decisions, and would usually consist of a sequence of decisions of the same type. To represent this we could better use an incidence matrix representation (see Table 1.3) which then gives us what is popularly known as a symbol-state table, or decision table.

The term 'decision table' is also, and more appropriately, used for another way of specifying an algorithm. A series of conditions $C_1, C_2 ..., C_m$ must be investigated to determine some choice among the actions $A_1, A_2, ..., A_n$. Usually the conditions C_i would 'test' one aspect of some data for one of many possible values, but without loss of generality we can assume that only binary conditions are used, as shown in Table 1.5. The table then represents a Boolean or Logical expression which can be converted into an optimal flowchart using the techniques of Boolean algebra. For a thorough treatment of decision tables, and their use in commercial computing, see the book by Humby.

	A_1	A_2	A_3	A_4	...	A_n
C_1	N	Y	Y	Y		N
C_2	N	Y	N	N		Y
...		...	...	...		...
C_m	Y	Y	Y	N		Y

Table 1.5. A binary decision logic table, with unspecified binary conditions C_1 to C_m, leading to actions $A_1, \ldots, A_n$. Note that $n \leq 2^m$. We could have $A_i = A_j$ for $i \neq j$. $N = $ NO, $Y = $ YES.

Many algorithms can be expressed very successfully using recursive statements. Recursive statements involve defining a problem in terms of smaller problems of the same type, with some 'stopping' condition in the form of trivial solutions to trivial problems. A classical example is factorial n: $n! = n \cdot (n-1)!$ with $0! = 1$. This is very readily converted into a graph algorithm (flowchart) involving a simple loop and no special storage. However, more complex recursions cannot simply be converted to a graph—extra storage in the form of a stack is required to 'track parameters'.

Let us now return to the tree traversals seen earlier in Algorithms 1.1 to 1.3. These were defined recursively, and we shall now consider removing the recursion. In Fig. 1.10 we see two versions in which the pre-order traversal is accomplished using a stack—in the second version, the stacking of empty trees has been avoided at the expense of a longer algorithm.

(a)

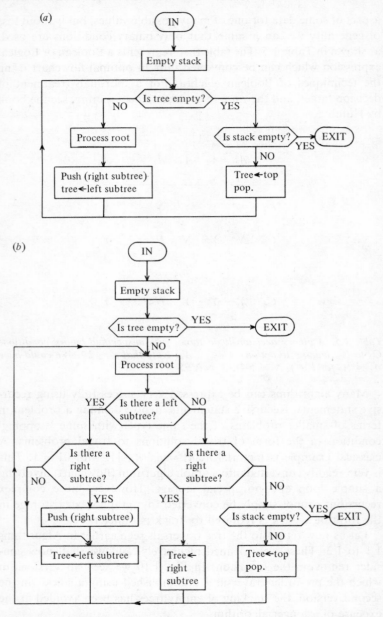

(b)

Fig. 1.10. Algorithm 1.4. Traversing a binary tree in pre-order. The stack retains the subtrees to be traversed later.

ABSTRACT INFORMATION AND ALGORITHMIC STRUCTURES

Stacks, or something equivalent, are essential in many algorithms, such as that for Ackerman's function (see Exercise 1.8.1). However, in other problems, such as tree traversal, stacks play a role of convenience rather than necessity. To see that stacks are not essential to tree traversal, consider the algorithm of Fig. 1.11, and contrast this

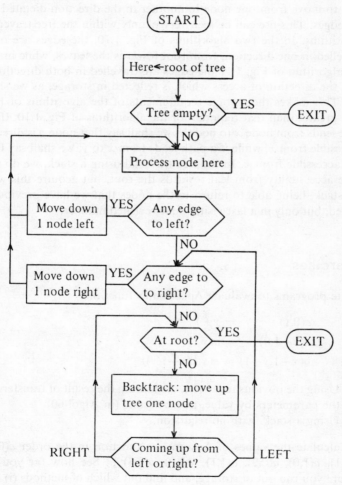

Fig. 1.11. Algorithm 1.5. Pre-order traversal of a binary tree, using bidirectional movements along the edges of the tree.

with the earlier algorithm for tree traversal in Fig. 1.10. The stack used in Fig. 1.10 provides an alternative and convenient way of 'backtracking' up the tree to a point you were at earlier.

We must now consider again graphs and trees in the context of algorithms. The directional property of the edges will be interpreted as a **direction of access**. During the execution of an algorithm we are able to move from one node to another in the direction dictated by the edges. This use can be seen very plainly within the tree traversal algorithms. In the two algorithms of Fig. 1.10, the edges are only travelled in one direction, from root towards the leaves, while in the the algorithm of Fig. 1.11 the edges are travelled in both directions. It is the direction of access which is reflected in storage, as we shall see. This makes the storage requirements of the algorithms of Fig. 1.11 greater than that required for the algorithms of Fig. 1.10. If an edge leads from node x to node y, we shall say that node y is **directly accessible** from x, while if a path leads from x to y, we shall say that y is **accessible** from x. In the tree traversal using a stack, we do not have accessibility from leaf towards the root, but acquire this with the stack, being able to return to the nodes that we have previously visited, but only in a last-visited-first-revisited manner.

1.8 Exercises

1.8.1 Write programs to evaluate Ackerman's function

$$a(0,y) = y+1$$
$$a(x+1,0) = a(x,1)$$
$$a(x+1,y+1) = a(x,a(x+1,y)).$$

(i) Using the obvious recursion, comparing the result of transferring the parameters by value, and by name (in Algol-60).
(ii) Using a stack, with no recursion.

Calculate the values of Ackerman's function in the order $a(0,0)$, $a(0,1)$, $a(1,0)$, $a(0,2)$, $a(1,1)$, $a(2,0)$, $a(0,3)$,.... See how far you get before you run out of storage, and find out which of methods (i) and (ii) is fastest. Try to find out why the one method is faster than the other.

.8.2 Draw flowcharts for algorithms to traverse binary trees in In-order and End-order, corresponding to the three methods we have seen for Pre-order traversals.

.8.3 Draw a flowchart to evaluate an arithmetic expression using a stack, but using no recursion.

.8.4 The following is an Algol-60 program for integrating a function of many variables (due to John Snell). It works recursively by subdividing the domain A of integration until it finds that two different simple estimates of the integral are 'good enough'. It is one of the few truly recursive numerical analysis methods. Program this (*a*) using a recursion, and (*b*) using a stack, and contrast the efficiency of the two solutions.

```
real procedure tree integral (f,A,m); value m; integer m;
    array A; procedure f;
    comment integrates f in domain A[1 : m];
    begin real x; x :=crude integral (f,A,m);
        if not good enough (x,f,A,m)
            then begin real array B(1 : m); integer i; x :=0 . 0;
                for i :=1 step 1 until number of parts do
                    begin partition (i,A,B,m); x :=x+tree integrals (f,B,m);
                    end;
                end;
            tree integral :=x;
        end of tree integral;
```

2 Machine structure: storage and control

In the previous chapter we considered computational problems in the abstract, carefully avoiding any assumptions about how we were to mechanise the problem solution. Ideally the machine's structure should match the problem's natural structure, but we shall see that this is often not the case with digital computers as they are currently manufactured—though the flexibility of the digital computer allows us to get round these restrictions without too much labour.

At this point we shall consider computers at the machine and assembly language level. High level languages, if appropriately designed, give the mechaniser of algorithms a more suitable machine, buffering him from the inadequacies of the basic machine. We shall assume here that the reader has some familiarity with the structure of digital computers and assembly language programming.

2.1 Storage structure

Let us first turn to the static aspects of the machine, the storage and its inherent structure. For us, storage will mean random access primary storage unless otherwise specified. This is usually core storage, though other methods are used. In later chapters on files we shall consider other storage and the restrictions their structure impose on the user.

A computer memory consists of a set of units which have addresses. These units could be words or bytes and will in turn be composed of typically between 8 and 48 bits. The addresses will be positive integers—and since there is a one to one correspondence between units and positive integers in some finite range through the addresses, this gives the storage a natural structure the same as that of the positive integers. The units have a natural ordering, are indexed, are adjacent if their addresses differ by one, and so on. That is the structure of the computer store as given to us by the engineers, and it is up to us to exploit its structure in the way we see fit.

The bits comprising the unit (its **contents**) can be interpreted by us in any way we like; as simply bit patterns, as codes for representing characters, as numbers either in a fixed point or floating point format, as instructions, or even as addresses. The hardware of the machine may cramp us in the way we interpret the bit patterns, but will not rule out any of the candidate interpretations. Different interpretations may, however, want more (or less) bits per unit than is wired in—thus we may want multi-unit storage **slots**. We shall be rather lax about terminology, and by context the interpretation of a collection of bits in a particular storage slot will be apparent, and hence its actual size in bits or storage units. We shall talk of storage slots as the basic components of storage, with addresses being the address of the first unit that makes up that slot, and whose contents are interpreted together in some manner.

If we choose a 'random' pattern of bits of the correct size, and interpret these as an address, we will access a random location or storage slot. We can do this over and over again, and thus use our memory in a **random access** manner. However, if we have an address, we could then increment by some fixed amount depending upon the size of our storage slot, and thus step through store by **sequential** or **serial** access. Random access use implies no structural relationships between slots, while serial access imposes the structure of a bi-directional linear tree.

1.1 Collections of storage slots

As we attempt to enrich our structural view of storage, the first thing that we shall want is to treat collections of slots as higher-order units This will be useful for indexed sets such as vectors, and matrices, for collections such as node descriptions, strings, and so on. The natural way to group together storage slots is to group together adjacent slots (though we shall see that this is not essential—the only important thing is that the grouping together should be manifest through the addresses). For these collections of slots we shall think of the address of a slot within a unit as being made up of two parts, one part of which selects the collection, and the other of which selects the slot within the collection. The two components of the address will be added together to give the actual address of the slot, thus:

$$\text{Address of slot} = \text{Address of} + \text{Address of slot}$$
$$\text{collection} \quad \text{relative to collection.}$$

If we are grouping together adjacent slots, we would normally consider the address of the collection as a base address, while the address of the slot relative to the collection is the offset, thus:

$$\text{Address of slot} = \text{base} + \text{offset.}$$

Collections of storage slots will be used in two important variations, which depend upon our way of interpreting the components of the collection.

We could wish to interpret all the slots in the same way, and step through the collection in some manner. We shall call such a collection a **vector** of storage. This is widely agreed terminology, and invariably the slots within a vector are adjacent, contiguous in storage.

In contrast, one may wish to interpret the storage slots within a collection differently, and only exceptionally step through them. Because of the different modes of interpretation, the slots would in general be of different size. We shall call such collections **records**, and the slots within the record being called **fields** (this terminology is by no means standard, being that used within the Pop-2 programming language, while in Algol-68 the records are called structs, and some authors call them nodes).

In many assembly languages, and most high-level languages, we are given a notation which will, in effect, do the address arithmetic for us. This allows us to write $X[R]$ where X is an address fixed when writing the program, and R is an address which is only determined during the execution of the program. In assembly languages this is called 'modification', and R would usually be a register whose value is added to the constant value X to determine an address. In high-level languages like Algol-60 or Fortran, these are arrays, and X is the name of the array or vector, and R is the index or offset. Both these devices have been designed for vector collections of storage, with X determining the collection and R determining the slot within the collection. Now we can turn this notation round and

24

exploit it for records! With records, we usually fix the field of the record when writing the program, but wish to make the record vary at execution time. So, in the notation $X[R]$ we let the X play the role of field selector, and let R be the variable record name. R is the collection name, and X determines the slot within the collection. We shall see this again in section 2.1.5. The significance of these remarks lies in the complimentary nature of records and vectors, and the fact that devices invented for vectors turn out to be very useful for records too.

.2 General relationships between slots using address arithmetic

We have seen that storage slots have addresses which are positive integers, and thus have the structure of the positive integers. We have exploited this fact in a small way in the last section when we joined slots together into larger collections thus relating slots which are contiguous in store. If we add two integers together we get a third integer which is an address.

But we can perform more elaborate calculations than simply addition, and can view addition in ways other than that used for collections of storage. Any relationships that we can invoke on the integers can be interpreted as a relationship between storage slots. The most important example for us will be a tree relationship for regular trees.

We can form up trees using address arithmetic in two ways. The first idea works for any amount of branching, but let us illustrate it with a binary tree. Suppose that we have a vector of storage A; we then set aside $A[1]$ to be the root of the tree, let $A[2]$ and $A[3]$ be its two descendants. In general we let $A[k]$ have descendants $A[2k]$ and $A[2k+1]$. Fig. 5.6 shows this. The tree we get is bidirectional because we can go from node $A[k]$ to its descendants by doubling k or doubling k and adding 1, but can also go back to the parent of $A[k]$ by halving k and losing the fractional part. We could have started with the root at $A[0]$, and that turns out to be easier for more general trees.

The other method using address arithmetic only works for binary trees. If we are using a vector of storage from slot i to slot j inclusive for the storage of a binary tree, then we make the root at slot

$m = \lfloor (i+j)/2 \rfloor$, the mid-point of the vector, with the subtree to the left of the root being stored in slots i to $m-1$ inclusive, and the subtree to the right of the root being stored in slots $m+1$ to j inclusive. This gives us a balanced binary tree, which is used for searching tables and similar problems. Two examples are given in Fig. 4.7 and discussed in section 4.1.2.1.1 on 'log search'.

By using tricks involving the properties of integers we could structure storage into simple graphs, cyclic stores, and so on. However, all these extensions are not adequate for the complex graphs that we shall want to store and manipulate, and we require greater flexibility in structuring storage. In the next section we shall see how to do this using a technique known as 'chaining'.

2.1.3 Relationships in storage using chaining

At the beginning of section 2.1 we emphasised the fact that the bit patterns in storage are at our disposal to be interpreted as we see fit. In particular we can interpret the bits as a positive integer which is an address. We can think of the address as **pointing** from one part of storage to another, thereby relating the first part of storage to the second. If the address pointer is part of one record, and points to a second record, we would say that the second is **linked** to the first. If we had a whole sequence of records linked in this way, we would then have a **chain**. Fig. 2.1 shows a chain of records. Note that at the end of the chain there is no linking pointer—in Fig. 2.1 this is symbolised by a cross where otherwise there is an arrow. We shall talk about the absence of a link as a **null pointer**, or simply as **nil**.

Fig. 2.1 shows the simplest form of chained structure, which is

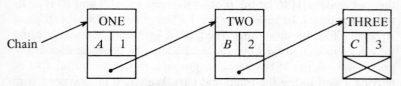

Fig. 2.1. A chain of records. Each box represents one record, with the divisions within the box showing the division of the record into fields. Where an arrow starts in a division, it means the field of the record is being interpreted as an address or pointer. The head of the arrow indicates the record pointed to by the field. A cross indicates a null pointer, which points nowhere.

known as a **linear list**. Other examples will be seen in Fig. 3.1(*d*) and Fig. 4.3(*c*). With linear lists we can represent linear trees in storage. The way we use them is to start at one end (the left in the diagrams) and move from record to record following the pointers. This is simple sequential access, and could also have been achieved using vector storage. But, as we shall see, chaining has its advantages.

Now in general we could have many pointers within a single record, and these could lead us anywhere within storage, including round in circles. We can use pointers for tying together small records of storage into larger units, and for representing the directed edges of graphs. Let us look at an example.

Fig. 2.2 shows a tree, and many alternative ways of representing this using chaining. We have by no means exhausted the possibilities. The general storage strategy is that within our program we are able to access the root of the tree—we have stored the address of the root, as indicated by the arrow which leads us into the top of the storage diagram. Then, starting at the record to which the incoming arrow takes us, we can move about the storage structure following pointers. But we cannot go backwards along pointers, and if we wish to backtrack, we must either store extra pointers to make the structure bidirectional, or we must use some other mechanism such as the stacks seen in the previous chapter.

Storage structures such as those of Fig. 2.2 are known by various names, from simply 'structures' in PL/I and Algol-68, to 'multi-linked lists' or the specially coined word 'plex'. We will usually refer to them by the generic term 'storage structure', the particular form of storage structure, whether chained, vector, address arithmetic, being clear from context.

From the example of Fig. 2.2 we can already note many of the aspects of the use of chaining, and also some of the difficulties. We will see a full graph example in a moment, but let us first list the various uses of pointers, and the problems arising from pointers.

These are:

(i) They dictate the direction of access. A pointer leads us into the structure, and from there on we can only move in the directions that the pointers take us. Thus in Figs. 2.2(*b*) and (*d*) we can only move away from the root towards the leaves, while in Figs. 2.2(*c*) and (*d*) we can start from any record and move to any other record by following an appropriate chain of pointers.

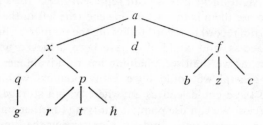

(a) The abstract tree.

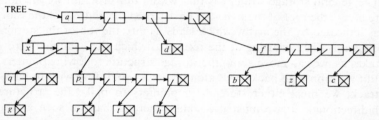

(b) A undirectional representation of the tree using two component records, where the first field is either a pointer or a node label, while the second component is always a pointer.

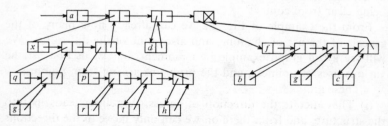

(c) A bidirectional representation, similar to (b), but using rings, closed cycles of pointers, to obtain the bidirectionality.

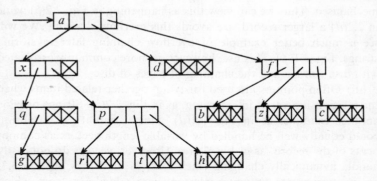

(d) *A undirectional representation of the tree, using records of a uniform size one data field and three pointer fields per record.*

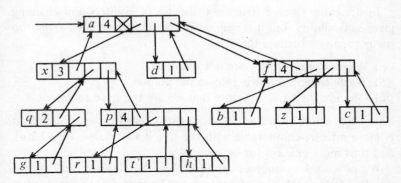

(e) *A bidirectional representation of the tree using records of variable size, with a precount to specify the number of pointers per record.*

Fig. 2.2. *An abstract tree, and various possible ways of representing it using chained storage. Note that in some variations the tree is represented unidirectionally, while in others the representation is bidirectional.*

(ii) Often pointers are used for tying together related items when the basic record size is not large enough for the problem being mechanised. Thus we can view this as happening in Fig. 2.2(*b*) while in 2.2(*d*) a larger record size avoids this **overflow** chaining. We will see a much better example of overflow chaining later in storing strings. Fig. 3.1(*f*). This use, however, is more commonly associated with disc storage and the chaining of pages of disc.

(iii) Often pointers are used for tying together related items when the relationship varies in extension, as in Fig. 2.2(*b*). Strings provide another example, as in Fig. 3.1(*d*). This variability in extension could equally well be handled by variable length vectors as components of the record, as in Fig. 2.2(*e*). However, vectors do not easily handle dynamically changing extensions, as in strings, section 3.3, or in storing sets to which elements are added, or from which elements are deleted.

(iv) Pointers are used to mirror directed edges of a graph or tree. A single edge of the graph may correspond to a single pointer, as in Figs. 2.2(*d*) and (*e*), or a single edge may correspond to a sequence of pointers as in Figs. 2.2(*b*) and (*c*), due to the use of pointers in roles (ii) and (iii) above.

In designing storage structures, the use of pointers and chaining gives us flexibility. But it is easy to overdo it, and we must avoid too many pointers, because these:

(i) Waste storage if they are not essential.
(ii) Waste time in following down the pointer.
(iii) Obscure the basic structure that we are trying to represent.

Fig. 2.2(*e*) is not only a more efficient structure for the computer, it is more directly comparable with the tree it represents, Fig. 2.2(*a*), and thus more efficient for us too.

We now look at another example. Fig. 2.3 shows a very simple graph of four nodes, part of a road-map. To represent this in storage, we could use two different records, and chain these together using pointers for tying towns to their roads, for tying the variable number of roads together, and for representing the edges of the graph, to show where the roads lead to. This structure, however, is not very satisfactory, for every road appears twice. Fig. 2.4 shows an alternative method. How this is arrived at will be explained in general terms later in the text.

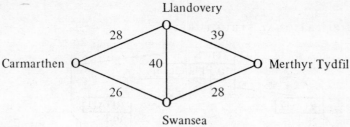

(a) The map.

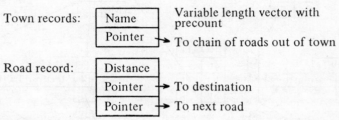

(b) The recores.

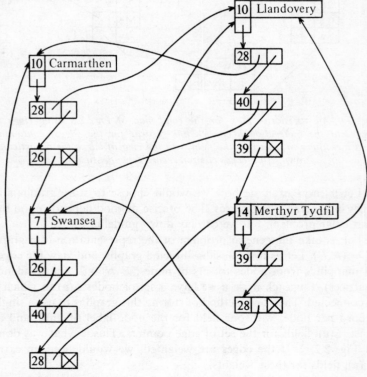

(c) The final structure.

Fig. 2.3. Representing a map using chaining.

31

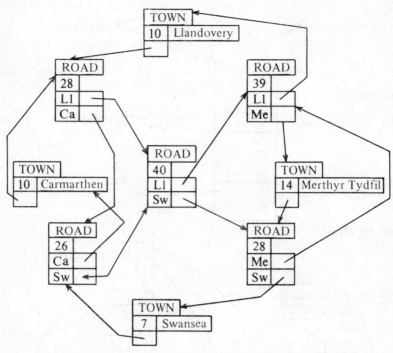

Fig. 2.4. An alternative plex for the road map of Fig. 2.3 using rings to represent the bidirectionality, with link-records for the edges, containing field identifiers to associate the field with the ring of edges for a particular town. All records contain record type identifiers.

Let us now examine how we would choose to store graphs and trees in general, using plexes. The precise method depends upon the particular problem, but we can lay down guidelines.

Let us take the general problem of the representation of a graph $G = (N,E)$. Let us first consider directed graphs, and view the edges as mappings from nodes to sets of nodes, $E:N \rightarrow 2^N$ (cf. incidence matrices). For each node **n** we have a set of nodes $E(\mathbf{n})$ to which **n** is connected. Then one method of storing this graph is to use a single record per node, with one field for the node label (if any), and at least $|E(\mathbf{n})|$ fields for the set of edge pointers. This is what was done in Fig. 2.2(*e*). If the edges are weighted, we would need an extra $|E(\mathbf{n})|$ fields for these weights.

We can, however, separate the node information from the edges information, using two records, one for the node, one for the edges, chaining these two records together, and could further separate the edges into a chained sequence with one record per edge, as we saw in Figs. 2.3(c) and 2.2(d).

For bidirectional graphs, we could use the strategy above, representing each direction quite independently, as in Figs. 2.2(e) and 2.3(c). But this can mean the duplication of information (in Fig. 2.3(c)), and worse, if we wish to change our graph during execution, we must change the graph in two places to maintain consistency. However, we can overcome this by exploiting rings. Now for every edge (**a,b**) we need a 'link record', storing in it a pointer which leads via other records to **a**, a pointer which leads via other records to **b**, plus additional fields for weights or labels if appropriate. The tree of Fig. 2.2(c) affords a simple example, but it takes Fig. 2.4 to show the real power (and problems) of this approach.

When following round the rings of Fig. 2.4, we cannot simply use the position of the field within the record to identify which pointer we want to follow to stay in the same ring, and thus must identify these with an extra field each—I have used the two initial letters of the town name for clarity, but clearly for road-maps this could fail. In rings, it is also conventional, and often very useful, to explicitly identify each node by its particular type, so that in following round a ring we know when we have completed the circuit. In Fig. 2.4 we see all these extra complexities, but this even so does provide a clearer representation of the graph. Contrast Figs. 2.3(c) and 2.4.

Within the last example we have seen several good ideas. One is to make the records in some measure 'self-describing', with fields to identify the type of the record, and other fields to indicate the meaning of particular fields. One idea only touched on was that of marking a 'head' position in a ring. In Fig. 2.4 this was done by encountering a record of different type as we traversed the ring. It is common, however, to set aside special records as 'ring-headers', and to use header records in other places, as a means for singling out common substructures that are easily changed, for enabling algorithms to be expressed more readily without having to treat the first record of a linear list as a special case. We shall see some examples in later chapters.

In practice, we may not be free to choose the best storage structure and may well be constrained by existing software to particular sub-sets of possibilities. The severest constraint will be imposed by storage management systems, the software or subprograms that look after the allocation of storage to particular uses, as records, or vectors, and so on. In section 2.1.4 we see how to write our own management systems, but in many high-level languages there is a built in storage management system, which in extreme cases could limit us to 'list' records of two fields each, which nevertheless might be worth using to save the problems of writing and debugging our own system.

2.1.4 Storage allocation and management

(*Note.* This section is primarily intended for reference, and no examples will be given to either motivate or illustrate the specific techniques. Full motivation and illustration will come later in the chapters on applications, when reference back to this section will be made.)

In this section we consider the problem of how we can set up in storage chained structures such as those we saw in section 2.1.3. If we know, when writing the program, precisely what the final structure will be, we can set up the structure by 'hand'. We simply set aside some contiguous storage, and allocate each record in turn to the next portion free in this area, and when all the records have been positioned in storage, we can replace the pointers by the appropriate addresses (or offsets). This is what was done in Fig. 2.5 for the storage structure of Fig. 2.3(*c*).

For large structures this hand mapping of the structure into storage involves a lot of work, but is perfectly adequate for structures which are fixed, such as the table of operation codes in an assembler, or the syntax specification graph in a compiler. However, when the structure is not going to be set up at program writing time, but will be formed during the **execution** of the program, as in the tables of user-defined symbols in an assembler, we must automate this storage allocation process.

There are two facets to storage allocation: one part is very problem dependent and relates to the order in which the records are considered for placement in storage; and the other is purely concerned with finding the next portion of storage available for a record. It is this second facet that is of principal interest here, and which we shall refer to as **storage management**.

100	101	102	103	104	105	106	107	108	109	110	111	112
10	CARM	ARTH	EN	105	28	111	108	26	125	0	10	LLAN

113	114	115	116	117	118	119	120	121	122	123	124	125
DOVE	RY	116	28	100	119	40	125	122	39	129	0	7

126	127	128	129	130	131	132	133	134	135	136	137	138
SWAN	SEA	135	14	MERT	HYR	TYDF	IL	138	26	100	141	39

139	140	141	142	143	144	145	146	147	148	149	150	151
111	144	40	111	147	28	125	0	28	129	0		

Fig. 2.5. Storage allocation by 'hand'. Allocation of storage to the structure of Fig. 2.3(c). The records have been allocated to storage slots starting at at address 100, storing one integer, one address, or four characters per slot.

In traditional high-level languages, such as Fortran and Algol-60, the use of storage is very restricted. In Fortran, the size of arrays must be decided once and for all when writing the program: the way the storage is apportioned between different uses cannot be made a function of the events which happen during the execution of the program, unless one adopts some low level techniques such as those given below. In Algol-60 the situation is only marginally better: one is allowed to dynamically obtain storage in variable amounts, and to return it for use later in some other manner, but this is restricted to a last obtained first released (a stack!) rule of storage use, determined by the block structure of the language.

In programming for general storage structures involving records, vectors, and chaining, we require complete flexibility to acquire storage slots in variable amounts, use these 'blocks' either as vectors or records, and to be able later to reuse the same area of store in some quite different manner, in blocks of a different size. We do not wish to be restricted as to the order in which storage is obtained and returned for reuse.

We shall assume that we have available a collection of storage slots (or words), STORE[1:N], with the ability to access these directly as STORE[i]. We shall assume that the value of N is fixed, and reflects all the storage available to our program. The objective will be to use portions of STORE[1 :N] in any capacity we desire, thinking of the blocks we obtain either as records or vectors as appropriate. We shall require:

(i) A method for remembering what portion of STORE[1 :N] is unused or **free**.
(ii) A routine for **acquiring** a portion of the free area for use within an applications program.
(iii) In some applications we shall require the ability to **return** storage that has been used to the free area for later reuse (this may be an explicit action, or it may happen implicitly through a **garbage collection**, as we shall see).

We shall see that it is comparatively easy to meet the requirements (i) and (ii), and often that is all that we need. It is requirement (iii) that introduces the problems, and we shall see essentially two distinct methods for handling this requirement for returning used storage to the free area: the first will be for records of a fixed and uniform size, while the second will be for records of a variable size.

Methods other than those given here, have been used for storage management. One body of methods uses 'usage counts' to determine when a portion of storage is no longer required. These are inferior methods. Another body of methods combine some of those that we will see below, so as to avoid the time required for garbage collection. In real time applications, when if storage is required, then it is required immediately, the delays of garbage collection are unacceptable.

Storage management routines should be implemented independently of any applications programs using those routines. **We can view our management routines as the building of a software machine or extending our programming language, so that we obtain a machine in which records are directly available.** After implementation of these routines, the applications package would be written at a higher level, referring only to records, and never referring directly to storage.

2.1.4.1 Acquire only

Here we only want to acquire storage from the free area, but never to return storage to the free area for reuse. The method is simple.

36

We maintain a variable FREE which indicates the lowest unused storage slot. Hence STORE[1 :FREE-1] has all been used, while STORE[FREE :N] is free and still available for use. This is shown diagrammatically in Fig. 2.6(a). We require two simple routines.

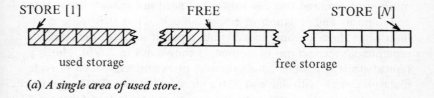

(a) *A single area of used store.*

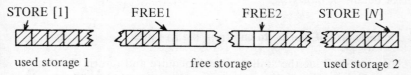

(b) *Two independent areas of used storage, but a single common free area.*

Fig. 2.6. *Simple acquire only storage management: the layout of storage.*

ROUTINES 2.1. *Storage management: acquire only*
1 Initialise;
  1.1 FREE ← 1;
  1.2. **Exit.**
2. Acquire(k);
  ¢ acquires a block of k slots from the free area ¢
  2.1. ¢ check if enough free storage left ¢
    if FREE+k > N **then** [¢ take error action ¢]
  2.2 ¢ return with the result a pointer to the new block ¢
    Result ← FREE;
  2.3. ¢ update free pointer ¢
    FREE ← FREE+k;
  2.4. **Exit.**

This gives us records or vectors of any size we need: a typical use could be

$$\text{NEW} \leftarrow \text{Acquire}(k);$$

whereafter to access the ith slot within this record, we would use STORE[NEW$+i$].

The same area of free storage could be used by many different processes and programs: this would lead to the storage being used for any particular purpose being intermingled with that used for other purposes, and this can make (but need not make!) the testing of programs and isolation of errors difficult. Thus it is quite common when there are only two distinct types of usage of the store, to separate out the sections of storage, as shown in Fig. 2.6(b). This is a typical strategy adopted, for example, in assemblers which provide macro facilities, with one end of the store being used for the symbol table, and the other end used for the macro table (see Chapter 4 for details of tables).

2.1.4.2 Uniform size of blocks, to and from the free area

Here we shall see the ability to both acquire and return blocks of a fixed uniform size k. Thus we shall assume that N is a multiple of k, $N = Mk$.

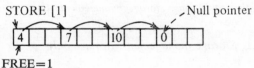

(a) *Actual storage contents.*

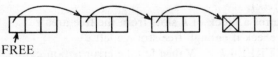

(b) *The logical organisation.*

Fig. 2.7. Chaining the free list in STORE [1:12], with four blocks of three slots each.

Now conceptually, STORE[1 :Mk] will be divided into M units, each of k storage slots. The jth unit is STORE $[(j-1)k+1 : jk]$. For the purposes of storage management, these blocks will be treated as records in which the first field is a pointer. These pointer fields will be used to chain together all the unused or free blocks into a **free-list**. Fig. 2.7 shows an example, where FREE is a pointer to the

38

beginning of the free-list chain. Note that the contents of the record, other than the first pointer field, are irrelevant. We shall require two basic routines, one for initially dividing up the whole of storage and setting up the free-list of M records, and a second for acquiring a record from the free-list. We shall also require two utility routines for accessing within the records, one to isolate the pointer field, and one to update the pointer.

These four routines are basic, and will be given first. The recovery of discarded storage can be done in one of two ways, depending on how much storage needs to be discarded at one go. If only single records are ever going to be discarded and returned to the free-list, the process can be a simple converse of the operation used to acquire the record; while if complete chained structures are to be discarded at one go, the best thing to do is to just lose them, and only recover them when there is no free storage left, in a phase known as **garbage collection**.

.2.1 *Basic routines*

These routines look after the manipulation of the pointer field within the records, used for chaining, and initialise the free list, and acquire new records from the free-list.

ROUTINES 2.2. *Free-list initialisation, and record acquisition.*
1. Next(REC);
   ¢ obtain the pointer from within the record REC, in the field in the first slot ¢
   1.1. **Result** ← STORE[REC];
   1.2. **Exit**.
2. Setnext(REC,P);
   ¢ sets the pointer field in record REC to pointer P¢
   2.1. STORE[REC] ← P;
   2.2. **Exit**.
3. Initialise;
   ¢ sets up the free-list and free-pointer, and the null-pointer ¢
   3.1. NIL ← 0;
   3.2. FREE ← 1;
   3.3. $p ← N−k+1$;

3.4. Setnext(p,NIL);
3.5. **while** [$p > 1$]
3.6.   **do** $_1$[$p \leftarrow p - k$;
3.7.   Setnext($p,p+k$);]$_1$
3.8. **Exit.**
4. Acquire;
  ¢ acquires the next record off the front of the free-list, returning a pointer to this as result ¢
4.1. **if** [FREE=NIL] **then** $_1$[¢ error—run out of storage ¢]$_1$
4.2.   **else** $_2$[**Result** ← FREE;
4.3.   FREE ← Next(FREE);]$_2$
4.4. **Exit.**

Very often the act of acquiring a record will also include the insertion into the fields in the record, values handed over as arguments. We shall see this later in notes on implementation, and within the applications that we shall study.

2.1.4.2.2 *Simple storage recovery*

We now come to the problem of how to return records of storage to the free-list, so that they may be used again later. The idea presented in this section is to return a single record to the free-list, placing the discarded record on the front of the free-list chain.

ROUTINES 2.3. *Simple free-list recovery of storage*
1. Return(REC);
  ¢ returns record REC to the free-list ¢
1.1. Setnext(REC,FREE);
1.2. FREE ← REC;
1.3. **Exit.**

In effect, the free-list forms a chained stack where the principle is Last Discarded, First Reused.

2.1.4.2.3 Complex storage recovery

In applications where large structures are made from the records using chaining (as in Figs. 2.2, 2.3, and 2.4), it may be necessary

40

to discard complete structures, or parts of structures, containing many records. This means returning to the free-list many records which may contain pointers to other records that are still wanted, and it is not easy to extend the simple principle of the last section for returning a single record to the free-list, to cope with large chained structures.

Accordingly, we now turn to quite a different method: during the execution of a program, we allow that records are discarded simply by updating pointers so that we no longer have any paths of access to these records (of course we can still get to them by accessing store directly). When the free-list becomes exhausted we then, and only then, gather together all the discarded records during a **garbage collection** phase.

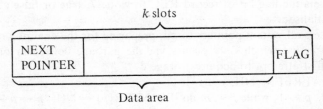

Data area

Fig. 2.8. Free-list garbage collection record structure. The NEXT-POINTER field is used only in the free-list, and can be used for other functions by the program, while the FLAG field of 1 bit is necessary for storage recovery in garbage collection, and cannot be used for data.

The technique for garbage collection is simple: mark the records that you still want, and then reconstitute the free-list from what is left.

To mark the useful records requires that we follow down all the pointers in the records, to wherever they lead, marking all the records on the way, until we either have come round in a circle to a record already marked, or have arrived at a point where there are no more pointers. We would have to start the marking process at standard 'pointer variables' which point into the chained storage area. To show that a record has been marked, an extra *flag* bit of storage will be required, and we shall assume that we have routines flag(.) and setflag(.,.). See Fig. 2.8 for a diagram showing the record structure.

41

Pointer variables will be taken as in a special vector of addresses, POINTER[1 : m].

In the routines that follow, we shall make further assumptions about the structure of the records for which the storage management system has been set up—in any real application, the principles will remain the same, but some of the detail may well differ.

ROUTINES 2.4. *Free list garbage collection system*
1. Next(REC); ¢ same as in Routines 2.2 ¢;
2. Setnext(REC,P); ¢ same as in Routines 2.3 ¢;
3. Flag(REC);
   ¢ accesses the flag bit of record REC, and returns with result **true** if the flag bit is set, **false** otherwise ¢;
4. Setflag(REC,T);
   ¢ sets the flag bit of record REC to value T, **true** or **false** ¢;
5. Initialise;
   ¢ sets all system pointers to nil, preparing for the chaining of the free-list which only occurs via the garbage collection on the first attempt to acquire storage ¢
   5.1. FREE ← NIL ← 0;
   5.2. p ← 1; **while** $p \leq m$ **do** [POINTER[p] ← NIL; p ← $p+1$;];
   5.3. p ← 1; **while** $p \leq N$ **do** [Setflag(p,**false**); p ← $p+k$;];
   5.4. **Exit.**
6. Acquire;
   ¢ acquires the next record from the front of the free-list ¢
   6.1. **if** FREE = NIL **then** [garbage collect];
   6.2. **Result** ← FREE;
   6.3. FREE ← Next(FREE);
   6.4. **Exit.**
7. Garbage collect;
   ¢ reconstitutes the free-list from storage that is no longer required ¢
   7.1. p ← 1; **while** $p \leq m$ **do** $_1$[Mark(POINTER[p]); p ← $p+1$;]$_1$;
   7.2. p ← 1; **while** $p \leq N$ **do**
   7.3. $\quad\quad$ $_2$[**if** flag(p) **then** [setflag(p,**false**)]
   7.4. $\quad\quad\quad\quad$ **else**[setnext(p,FREE); FREE ← p;]
   7.5. $\quad\quad$ p ← $p+k$;]$_2$
   7.6. **if** FREE = NIL **then** [¢ error—run out of storage ¢];
   7.7. **Exit.**

8. Mark(P);

¢ marks the chained structure pointed to by P, following down pointers within records recursively ¢

8.1.   **if not**(P = NIL **or** flag(P)) **then**

8.2. $_1$[Setflag(P,**true**);

8.3.   ¢ follow all the pointers within this record: we shall assume that first K slots, with $k > K$, are pointer fields. These could be null. Other conventions could allow a field to contain either data or a pointer, with means of distinguishing between these ¢

$j \leftarrow 0$; **while** $j < K$ **do** [Mark(STORE[$P+j$]);]

]$_1$

8.4. **Exit**.

.3 Variable size records, to and from the free area

If the size of records to be obtained from, and returned to, the free area are of variable size, we are unable to use the techniques of section 2.1.4.2, and must extend the ideas of section 2.1.4.1 for acquisition only.

The method that we shall consider will involve garbage collection, only gathering together storage that has been discarded, once the current free area has been exhausted. The free area will be maintained at the upper end of STORE, as in Fig. 2.6(a), but now we shall require extra storage attached to each record to assist the recovery of discarded storage. Fig. 2.9 shows the record structure that we will require, with four fields to assist recovery. The first field, SIZE, records how large the block of storage that follows is, to enable us to step through STORE from record to record. The second field, NEXT POSITION, is for temporary storage when we plan the movement of the useful records down storage, the third field, RECORD TYPE, enables us to identify the pointer fields within the record, while the fourth field, FLAG, plays the same role as in the free-list garbage collection, to mark useful storage, to distinguish this from the garbage.

The general idea is to mark the useful storage that must be retained, and then move the useful storage down store to close the gaps left by the garbage, to eventually return to the position of Fig. 2.6(a).

43

Because we are moving data about storage, changing its address, we must update all pointers. There are four stages.

(i) Mark all those records which are accessible via the standard base pointers.

(ii) Scan storage, moving from record to record, working out where each record will be shifted to when we close up the gaps left by the garbage, using the field NEXT POSITION to retain this information in the record.

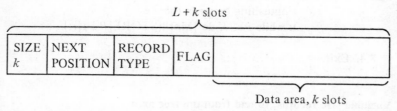

Fig. 2.9. Variable size record storage management: the record structure. The four fields at the start of the record are a fixed overhead per record.

(iii) Scan storage, moving from record to record, taking every pointer contained within the record, following it to the record to which it points, and then updating the pointer using the value in NEXT POSITION; also update all the standard base pointers.

(iv) Shift the marked records down storage to close up the gaps, unmarking the records after shifting; set FREE to point just above the last record moved.

ROUTINES 2.5. *Variable size record storage management*
1. Size(REC); ¢ obtain SIZE field within record REC ¢.
2. Setsize(REC,V); ¢ set the SIZE field of record REC to value V ¢.
3. Next(REC); ¢ obtain NEXT field within record REC ¢.
4. Setnext(REC,A); ¢ set the NEXT field within record REC to value (address) A ¢.
5. Type(REC); ¢ obtain TYPE field within record REC ¢.
6. Settype(REC,T); ¢ set TYPE field within record REC to value T ¢.
7. Flag(REC); ¢ obtain FLAG field within record REC ¢.
8. Setflag(REC,F); ¢ set FLAG field within record REC to value (logical) F ¢.

44

9. Initialise;
   9.1. FREE $\leftarrow$ 1; NIL $\leftarrow$ 0;
   9.2. ¢ set L to number of slots used for work fields ¢.
   9.3. $p \leftarrow$ 1; **while** $p \leq m$ **do** [POINTER[p] $\leftarrow$ NIL; $p \leftarrow p+1$;];
   9.4. **Exit.**

10. Acquire(k,t);
   ¢ acquires a block of k slots from free area, adding L extra
   slots for the extra fields SIZE, NEXT, TYPE, FLAG ¢
   10.1. **if** FREE$+k+L > N$ **then** [garbage collect(k)];
   10.2. **Result** $\leftarrow$ FREE;
   10.3. Setsize(FREE,k); Setflag(FREE,**false**); (FREE,t);
   10.4. FREE $\leftarrow$ FREE$+k+L$;
   10.5. **Exit.**

11. Garbage collect(k);
   ¢ identifies the useful storage and thus the garbage, then plans
   the moves, updates the pointers and then moves the records to
   occupy the space left by the garbage ¢
   11.1. ¢ mark the storage that is still useful ¢
      $p \leftarrow$ 1; **while** $p < M$ **do** $_1$[Mark(POINTER[p]);
                                      $p \leftarrow p+1$;]$_1$;
   11.2. ¢ plan moves ¢
      $q \leftarrow$ 1; $p \leftarrow$ 1; **while** $p <$ FREE **do**
   11.3. $_2$[**if** Flag(p) **then**
   11.4. $_3$[Setnext(p,q); $q \leftarrow q+$Size(p)$+L$;]$_3$
   11.5. $p \leftarrow p+$Size(p)$+L$;]$_2$
      ¢ q retains the value to which FREE will later be adjusted ¢
   11.6. **if** $q+k+L > N$ **then** $_4$[¢ catastrophe, store full; take
                                 error action ¢]$_4$;
   11.7. ¢ update all pointers ¢
      $p \leftarrow$ 1; **while** $p \leq m$ **do** $_5$[POINTER[p] $\leftarrow$
                              Next(POINTER[p]);]$_5$
   11.8. $p \leftarrow$ 1; **while** $p <$ FREE **do**
   11.9. $_6$[**if** Flag(p) **then** $_7$[¢ locate all pointer fields in record p
          using TYPE(p), and update these by following down
          the pointer and using the NEXT field of the record
          to which it leads ¢]$_7$
   11.10. $p \leftarrow p+$Size(p)$+L$;]$_6$
   11.11. ¢ shift records down to close the gaps left by garbage ¢
      $p \leftarrow$ 1; **while** $p <$ FREE **do**

11.12. $_8$[if Flag(p) then

11.13. $_9$[$t \leftarrow 0$; while $t \leq$ Size(p)+L do

$_{10}$[STORE[Next(p)+t] $\leftarrow$ STORE[p+t];

$$t \leftarrow t+1;]_{10}$$

11.14. Setflag(p,**false**);]$_9$

11.15. $p \leftarrow p$+Size(p)+L;]$_8$

11.16. ¢ adjust FREE pointer ¢

FREE $\leftarrow q$;

11.17. **Exit.**

12. Mark(P);

¢ marks the chained structure referenced through pointer P, following down pointers within records recursively, until either a record already marked is reached, or a null pointer is met ¢

12.1. **if not** ($P =$ NIL **or** Flag(P)) **then**

12.2. $_1$[Setflag(P,**true**);

12.3. ¢ follow all pointers within record P by using Type(P) to identify the pointers, and then marking the records these point to recursively. We shall assume here, for illustration, that Type (P) indicates the number of leading fields which are pointers ¢

$j \leftarrow 0$; while $j <$ Type(P) do

[Mark(STORE[P+L+j])]]$_1$

12.4. **Exit.**

2.1.5 Implementation techniques for records

In the previous sections on storage management we saw, in effect, one device for naming fields within a record. This was through function calls, and we now consider alternative methods which exploit the facilities available in common programming languages.

With function calls, we gave the name of a record (a pointer) as argument to a function whose name identified the field. To update the same field required a second subroutine of two arguments, and let us now consider alternatives to this. Very commonly on acquiring a record, we want immediately to fill in values in all the fields, and to use field updaters is laborious. This suggests that our acquire routine should include field initialisation, and thus a common practice is the following, to replace Acquire.

ROUTINES 2.6. *Record constructor*

1. Cons($a_1,a_2,...,a_k$);

¢ constructs a record, obtaining the record from the free-list, and then filling in values in the k fields ¢

   1.1. **if** FREE = NIL **then** [garbage collect];

   1.2. **Result** ← t ← FREE;

   1.3. FREE ← Next(FREE);

   1.4. STORE[t] ← a_1;

   ... ...

   1.3+k. STORE[$t+k-1$] ← a_k;

   1.4+k: **Exit**.

With the facility to construct records, updating fields often becomes unnecessary, and indeed undesirable. Updating fields can have side effects, altering other structures in an unexpected way, and so if we want a modified version of a record, a new record would normally be constructed with field values filled in from the old record where necessary.

The use of functions or routines to name fields within a record is not the only device that can be exploited. Indeed, in assembly languages this could be a very inconvenient method. When discussing records in section 2.1.1, we suggested that the indexing mechanisms of both assembly and high-level languages, designed for vector storage, could very usefully be exploited for records, placing the record name (pointer) in the index position, and the field name in the base position, thus FIELD[RECORD]. Now the component fields of a record do not have to be contiguous in storage, and so we can define, in Fortran or Algol-60 for example, a **separate array for each field**, associating the array elements of the same index into a single record.

For example, suppose we desire records composed of four fields, LEFT, KEY, ENTRY, and RIGHT, we could then declare arrays of the appropriate type: LEFT[1 : M], KEY[1 : M], ENTRY[1 : M], and RIGHT[1 : M], and for the purposes of management set aside one of these for chaining the free-list. Record R would then comprise storage slots LEFT[R], KEY[R], ENTRY[R], and RIGHT[R]. This technique for storing records allows assignments both ways, and leads to programs that are easy to read.

In the management routines, we required a FLAG field of a single

47

bit—this is most readily made the sign bit of a pointer field (pointers would be positive), when setting the flag means changing the sign from positive to negative.

2.1.6 Storing abstract structures

In this section we will consider how to store the abstract structures that we studied in Chapter 1. Mostly we will be gathering together methods that we have already seen earlier in this chapter, at the same time referring ahead to later chapters where some facets will be covered in greater detail. We will also see one or two new ideas.

2.1.6.1 Storing sets

Sets are the simplest kind of structure that we encountered. For storing sets, there are two basic approaches. We can
either (I) for each set store details about every element actually in the set, as one does in writing down the elements of a set contained between braces;
or (II) we identify every potential element of the set, and then for each subset of this universal set, we indicate for every potential member of the set, whether this is actually in the set or not.

For Method I we can use either a vector or a linear list to store the elements. Fig. 2.10(*a*) and (*b*) illustrate the idea. Typical operations on the sets would be to find out whether a particular item is in the set or not, to add new items to the set, to remove items from the set, and to perform the usual set-theoretic operations such as the union or intersection of two sets. Operations involving a single item and the set takes us into tables, and the methods of Chapter 4 are relevant. Set operations like union and intersection benefit greatly from having the sets ordered, and for these simple sequential tables as in section 4.1.1 are ideal, using the merge ideas of section 4.2.1 for performing the actual operations.

The alternative Method II indicates for each potential member of the set whether or not the element is actually in the set. We number all the potential members of the set from 1 to N, and then set aside a storage vector of N **bits**, and store the set by setting the ith bit to 1 (true) if the ith potential element is in the set, and to 0 (false) otherwise. Fig. 2.10(*c*) illustrates this when $N = 26$. If N is very large,

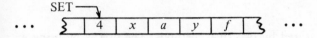

(a) *Method I, using a vector.*

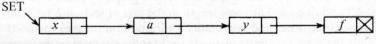

(b) *Method I, using a linear list.*

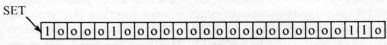

(c) *Method II, using a bit vector of 26 components.*

Fig. 2.10. Storing a set. An example illustrating the methods, for the set $\{x, a, y, f\}$ where there are 26 possible members, the small letters of the alphabet.

and in applications such as information retrieval (see section 4.3) N could be greater than 100,000, this method involves a tremendous amount of storage. If the number of elements in any individual set is small, then we could far more efficiently store only those elements that are present, using Method I. The great attraction of Method II using bit vectors is that the set operations of union and so on can be done **very** effectively using machine-level logical operations on machine words viewed as bit vectors.

Notice that once stored, the sets obtained an indexing from their method of storage, the different methods of storage enabling this indexing to be exploited in different ways. Very often any total ordering of the set occurring naturally is used, and the set is kept sorted. We shall see a variety of methods for sorting sets in Chapter 5.

.2 Storing strings

Strings can be stored either using vectors or chaining. In Chapter 3 the alternative methods for the storage of strings are considered in great detail. Fig. 3.1 shows various possibilities.

49

3

2.1.6.3 Storing graphs

Graphs can be stored by two rival methods. The first is by using a matrix, either the connection or incidence matrix of Tables 1.2 and 1.4, storing the matrix in a vector in the standard way. The alternative is to use a plex, representing the edges of the graph by pointers, as in Fig. 2.3 and discussed at some length in the text of section 2.1.3. The incidence matrix method is in reality a variation on the plex method!

Thus there are two basic methods for graphs; connection matrices and plexes. Which is appropriate depends primarily upon the number of edges. For N nodes, there are $N(N+1)/2$ possible edges, and if the actually number of edges is much less than this, then the connection matrix would be sparse, and much storage would be wasted; a plex would be preferable. However, for some operations on graphs, the connection matrix is most convenient, since the operations reduce to matrix operations.

2.1.6.4 Storing trees

We saw that trees are a special kind of graph, and thus the methods used for graphs could also be used for trees. However, connection matrices are not used for trees, because the matrices are sparse, having non-zero entries only in the upper-triangular half of the matrix. Chained storage is used almost always, and we saw a series of examples in Fig. 2.2. With chained storage the edges or branches of the tree are explicitly represented by pointers. We also saw an alternative method in which the edges were implicitly understood through address arithmetic. This method is used within some table and sorting techniques.

2.1.6.5 Storing stacks

The final structure that we will need to be able to represent in storage is the stack. We have two methods for this; using a vector with a 'stack pointer' which is incremented or decremented as items are placed on the stack and removed from the stack, as in Fig. 2.11(a); and using a linear list, placing new storage records on the front of the list, or removing records from the front of the list, as the stack is added to or reduced, as in Fig. 2.11(*b*). Most commonly the vector form would be used, but this does have disadvantages. A maximum size of stack has to be decided upon while writing a program, and storage used for the stack cannot be freely traded for storage for other purposes during program **execution**. The linear list method for

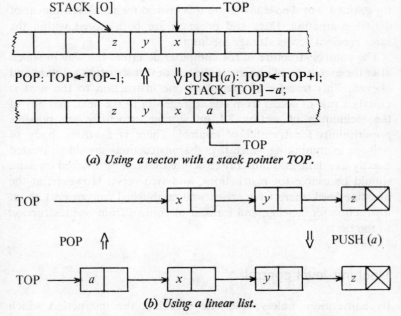

STACK [O]

TOP

POP: TOP←TOP−1; ⇑   ⇓ PUSH(*a*): TOP←TOP+1;
STACK [TOP]←*a*;

TOP

(*a*) *Using a vector with a stack pointer TOP.*

TOP

POP ⇑   ⇓ PUSH (*a*)

TOP

(*b*) *Using a linear list.*

Fig. 2.11. *Two methods for storing a stack, as in Fig. 1.9.*

stacks does permit the dynamic trading of one form of storage against another, without the need to know beforehand how large the stack might become. Very often the items being stored on the stack will be 'bulky', may vary in size, and the overhead of the pointer will be negligible. If a general purpose storage management system is available to you (see section 2.1.4: you may have written the routines yourself, or they may be available to you as part of the programming system that you are using, such as Algol-68 or PL/I) then using a linear list as a stack would involve no more effort than using a vector.

51

2.2 Control structures

We have studied storage, its natural structure, and the way this can be exploited to enable us to store and manipulate trees and graphs. The computer program, the instructions telling the computer what to do, is itself held within the random access core storage of the computer. This is the **stored program concept** which today is taken for granted, but whose invention was critical for the development of digital computing. Data and program are both stored within the same random access storage medium.

The control structure of the computer describes the way in which after the execution of one instruction, a next instruction is found and obeyed. This **transfer of control** of one instruction to the next is exactly a rule of access from one storage slot to the next, and any of the techniques of section 2.1 on storage structures are possible prescriptions for transfer of control. There is a strong body of opinion in computing which says that instructions should be treated exactly like data, and thus any structure that can be invoked on data, should be usable for instructions, and vice versa. However, at the machine level, there have arisen well-established conventions about instruction sequencing, and transfer of control from one instruction to the next.

2.2.1 Machine-level control

By convention, unless otherwise specified, the instruction which follows that at slot A, is that at slot $A+1$. This is the sequential rule of access, structuring the store as a linear tree. Of course this is totally inadequate for algorithms, but it is a good start. (*Note.* Storage slots for machine instructions are, in most digital computers, all of the same size. However, in some computers, different instructions may require different size slots, and some computers even allow automatic features to mix data and instructions. By slot $A+1$ I mean the next instruction slot on, which, when one takes into account these complexities, may be as many as six or eight machine words on in core storage.)

Departures from the sequential rule for instruction sequencing are made then by special **instructions** in a way that is very similar to the use of 'escape' characters in character codes. These special transfer of control instructions break the default sequence. The simplest form is the unconditional jump or branch—a new starting point is indicated within the instruction and control is transferred to that point. The address given (it most likely will be a 'relative' address, that is an offset from the current instruction address) is the address of the next instruction. The important use of unconditional jumps is to close loops of instructions, to allow repetitive operations. Unconditional jumps are also used to jump round data, but that use is irrelevant for us here.

The crucial transfer of control is the conditional transfer. In its simplest form this is the conditional jump—the instruction specifies an address, and if a designated bit is a one (or if some logical computation on several bits yields a result of one), the control is transferred to the specified address, otherwise control transfers to the next instruction in the 'normal' way. A variation on this conditional jump is the skip instruction—if some condition is met, the next instruction is skipped—when, for a conditional branch, the skipped instruction is made an unconditional branch. Usually the conditions on which the instructions operate are phrased in an arithmetic manner, as the sign of a number, or the value of a number: this indicates the heaviness with which numerical processes sit upon digital computing, but does not change the essentially bit manipulation and inspection nature of the conditions.

Conditional jumps and skip instructions enable us to make simple two way branches, one of which continues the normal sequence, while the other breaks out of the normal sequence. Multi-way branches can be readily programmed using 'jump tables', or 'switches': at their simplest these would take the form of a vector of addresses, and after the calculation of some offset I, the Ith address within the vector is obtained, and control transferred to that point. More complex strategies would maintain a table in which a match of keys is sought and thus an address found, which is then used as the transfer address (see Chapter 4 on tables). Only seldom are multiway branches best implemented using sequences of conditional branches.

The control structures so far seen, unconditional jumps, condtional jumps, skips, and switches, are sufficient for implementing any algorithm. But they force us into using a non-hierarchically expressed algorithm. Assembly languages allow one control structure which greatly facilitates the hierarchical implementation of algorithms. This is the subroutine. From the machine point of view, the importance of subroutines is that they allow the sharing of program coding, thus saving storage. From the user point of view, they allow the sharing of effort—a subroutine developed today, can be used next year within a different problem—and even more importantly, enable the programmer to express his algorithms in a hierarchical manner, coding and testing subalgorithms independently. Subroutines (and macros, see later paragraphs) are not enough for the proper hierarchical expression of algorithms, but they are an essential first step, and one that is supplied in all computer machine languages. More advanced hierarchical features would permit full statement nesting, and block structures, at present associated mostly with some high-level languages.

Subroutines provide the programmer with the ability to transfer control from one part of storage to another, and later on **return to the instruction following the initial transfer.** This leads to special subroutine linkage instructions, with two instructions, one for jumping to the subroutine while remembering where the transfer was made from, and the other for using the return address in order to return from the subroutine. This is a master–slave relationship, a true hierarchy, and moving between levels in the hierarchy by anything other than the proper linkage instructions must be viewed as very bad practice. At the machine level, such bad practice is permitted, though it can indirectly lead to catastrophe; happily, most high-level languages do not even permit such evils. Usually machine-level subroutine calls cannot be cyclic, not allowing recursion. Often the extent to which subroutines can call other subroutines, and so on, is also severely restricted. The transfer of data during subroutine linkage is also important, and facilities vary tremendously.

A useful extension of the subroutine idea is the **co-routine.** These are two or more routines which co-operate on an equal status, rather than the master–slave relationship of subroutines. Each co-routine can invoke another co-routine as necessary—a typical use of co-routines would be for input, for processing, and a third for output. Some computers include special facilities which enable co-routines to be written simply and efficiently.

An increasingly common feature of assembly languages, and also high-level languages, is **macros**. These are not properly to be regarded as control structures, but must be discussed at this point since they are complimentary to subroutines and provide the programmer with the same facility for the hierarchical expression of algorithms. Macros allow the programmer to use shorthand when writing his program; then in a pre-pass through his program text **before** assembly, the shorthand macros are **expanded** to the full sequence of text and machine operations that they summarise. While the macro idea can be treated as a text manipulation capability, the way in which they appear in assembly languages makes them very closely equivalent to subroutines, with an operation being specified by name, with additionally some arguments. Logically they are very close, but at the machine level they are very different, for each use of a macro leads to the complete generation of coding for that operation, and there is no sharing of code. After macro expansion, the hierarchical decomposition of the algorithm largely disappears, and is completely absent at execution. The choice as to which to use, macro or subroutine, depends upon trade-offs between space-saving and time-taken for subroutine linkage.

We have seen at the machine level the structures that are made available to the programmer for controlling his program. These do not exploit the full potential of core storage structures, but rather rest upon long established convention. These allow the programmer to realise within his program an arbitrarily complex algorithm graph, but does not allow much flexibility in expressing the algorithm hierarchically. Only in the latest high-level languages have anything like adequate capabilities in this direction been given.

.2 High-level control

The machine-level structures that we have studied in the preceding section are sufficient for the mechanisation of algorithms, but are not really adequate. Programming in assembly or machine language is tedious, partly because the basic operations for doing work at the assembly level are very primitive, but also in part because the facilities for controlling the sequence of operations is also very primitive.

High-level languages arose as a way of making the computing machine more suited to the problems that it was used for. Let us see what they offer for controlling a mechanical process or routine.

Firstly, the methods at the machine level for supplying arguments or parameters to subroutines is often very contrived, and a first improvement is to enable one to use conventions like those used in mathematics, to refer to a subroutine by name, with any parameters following the name enclosed by brackets. This improvement was done very early on, in Fortran, but an artificial distinction was made between subroutines which had no implicit answer to deliver, and functions which had a single implicit answer to deliver. More recent languages try to unify these two concepts.

Repeating an operation, or a sequence of operations, some pre-determined number of times, is a very basic requirement in computing, that was also recognised early on in the Fortran DO-loop. This is as far as Fortran progressed, and so in many ways Fortran is an assembly language. Repetitions controlled by a single count are far from adequate, for we often wish to repeat something until some logical condition has been met, as in summing a series of numbers until the numbers we are adding in become insignificantly small, or in searching through a collection of items until we find the one we are looking for, or exhaust the collection and know that the item is not there. This has led to various constructions for controlling repetitions, such as **while** ⟨condition⟩ **do** and **until** ⟨condition⟩ **do**, these being combined with the counting form of repetition into a single repeat facility, with varying degrees of success. (Algol-60 tries, but fails, here.)

To allow sequences of operations to be joined together and treated, for the purposes of control, as a single operation, we must be able to bracket together sequences of operations into a 'compound' operation. This is one function of the **begin end** pair in Algol-60, and is essential for a flexible control capability.

When we ask a question about something within an algorithm, it is not so much that we wish to jump to another part of our algorithm (that is a very machine-level, storage-conscious, idea), but rather that we wish to perform one sequence of operations if some condition is met, and some other sequence of operations otherwise. This leads to the construction **if** ⟨condition⟩ **then** ⟨compound operation⟩ **else** ⟨compound operation⟩. But such a two way interrogation of a condition is not enough, and often we wish to look at several different cases, taking different actions as appropriate. This can be done using

if's nested inside each other, or extensions of the **if** idea using contractions like **elseif** and **thenif**, but these are not completely adequate, and the construction invented for multiway conditions is the **case** construction of Algol-68 and other languages.

With the general conditional and repetition constructions, and the use of statement brackets to compound operations, we now have acquired some new and important capabilities for the hierarchical expression of our algorithms. Now subprocesses will nest inside the larger process, and this relationship will be apparent on looking at the control aspects of the program. These subprocesses can be made to be immediately apparent by the way we graphically present our program, by using indenting to emphasise nesting so that, **at a glance**, the hierarchical structure of a program can be appreciated. Since the hierarchical structure is manifest in the control, this display can be mechanised, and any good compiler for modern high-level languages should do the indenting to display the program for easy reading.

Making programs easy for humans to read is very important, but there is one control facility that has been carried over from the machine level, and which makes programs unnecessarily difficult to read. This is the **goto** command. The perniciousness of the **goto** was first analysed by Dijkstra: the use of a **goto** completely foils all our attempts at making the paths of control, and the hierarchical structure of a program, immediately appreciated. The only way to sort out what is happening is to in effect **obey** the program, follow the **goto** to where it leads, with all the hard work that that entails.

In this book I have tried to use control constructions that will be immediately obvious to all readers. I have used [ ] as statement brackets (and also for subscripts, but that should not prove confusing), and have used a single form of repetition, a **while do** construction. A standard **if then else** conditional is used, though at times I wished that I had standardised on a more general **case** construction. Subroutine linkage is almost standard, with parameters enclosed in brackets following the subroutine name, but for returning results from a subroutine I have assigned the results to the standard variable **Result**, intending that this should be obvious on reading. In one or two instances results have been returned via parameters, and in one or two cases more than one result has been returned by assignment to **Result1, Result2,** and so on. **Goto**'s have been (almost) completely avoided, though in some instances I have been a small bit fraudulent! In some routines I have used an **Exit** deep down in the hierarchy: this could have been avoided, and you are invited to make the changes yourself. Lines in the routines have been numbered. These are not statement labels, but are used for referring to the steps within the routines in other routines and in discussions in the text.

2.3 Exercises

2.3.1 Program a knockout tournament among a random set of numbers $\{a_1, a_2, ..., a_n\}$, where the winner of a 'game' is the larger of a pair of numbers. Program the tournament by setting up a binary tree in an array $b[1 : 2n-1]$ using address arithmetic for computing the edges of the tree, with $b[k]$ having descendents $b[2k]$ and $b[2k+1]$. The numbers $\{a_1, ..., a_n\}$ start in $b[n], ..., b[2n-1]$, and at the end of the tournament the largest number ends up at the root of the tree, at $b[1]$.

Could you extend your program so that it will select the second largest number using only $\log_2 n$ comparisons (you will have used $n-1$ comparisons in finding the largest)? Could you then continue to the third largest number, and so on, so that eventually you have selected all the numbers in descending order, and thus have sorted them? To do this you will require some chaining as well. For a complete solution, see 'treesort', Algorithm 113, in the *Communications of the ACM* (August 1962), p. 434. This is quite a good method for sorting numbers, but we will see much better methods in Chapter 5.

2.3.2 Write a program which will read in data consisting of four-letter mnemonics and a number, storing these in a linear chained sequence of records

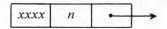

with three fields, Mnemonic, Number, and Next. Maintain the sequence sorted by mnemonic (thus, AAAA is first and ZZZZ is last). As each new pair of data items are read in, and a new record obtained, this record should be inserted into the correct position in the chained sequence. After reading in all the data, it should be printed out sorted by mnemonic—the original data would have been in random order.

[*Note*. if you are using a traditional high-level language like Basic, Fortran, or Algol-60, use arrays MNEM[1 :N], NUM[1 : N], NEXT[1 : N] so that record R has fields MNEM[R], NUM[R], and NEXT[R]. Only the simplest form of management is necessary.]

.3 Extend the program of 2.3.2 so that

(i) If a mnemonic appears twice, the second occurrence updates the first number entered against that mnemonic, with no new record being created.

(ii) If a mnemonic appears with the number 0 associated, then the record for that mnemonic is deleted.

This second part requires a full storage management system allowing the returning of discarded records to the free area of store. Full garbage collection is not required.

.4 Arrange a storage management system for labelled binary trees using records with fields Left, Value, and Right. Use this for storing the binary trees of algebraic expressions, arranging that the expressions can be read in as data in **forward polish** notation, and after the tree has been formed, the expression can be written out correctly bracketed infix notation, and in reverse polish, by traversing the tree in the appropriate manner.

If recursion is not available in the language that you are using, then you may require a stack (with clever programming you can avoid the need for the stack). Program your stack using linear lists.

.5 Implement a full list-processing system: a list-processing system is a programming system in which records are available in a very restricted form. Each record has two fields only, called HEAD and TAIL respectively. The HEAD field can contain data or pointers, while the TAIL field must be a pointer (or the null pointer). A full account of list-processing is given in the book by J. M. Foster: make your implementation compatible with his notation, accessing the record fields via procedures, with procedures TAIL( ), SETTAIL( ), HEAD( ), SETHEAD( ), and CONS(,) together with full garbage collection as detailed in section 2.1.4.2.3. Note that there are difficulties if garbage collection occurs during recursion.

2.3.6 Consider all the programming languages that you know, and compare them critically with respect to control structures. Which has the richest set? Which is 'best'?

2.3.7 If you have access to a language with macro facilities (this will most likely be an assembly language) experiment to see whether you can extend the control structures of the language using macro substitutions. What you can do in this direction will depend very much upon the restrictions within the macro facility that you are using.

2.3.8 Express the bidirectional tree traversal of Fig. 1.11 using the control structures of this book; that is, using **while do** and **if then else** constructions only, without any **goto** statements. If you have access to a programming language with the right control structures (such as Algol-68 or PL/I) try programming the tree traversal using **gotos** in the obvious way following Fig. 1.11, and without using **gotos**. Try to assess which method leads to the fewest mistakes in programming, and which method is easiest to explain to another programmer.

3 String processing

As a first series of examples in non-numerical computing, let us study problems involving strings. We shall consider quite a large range of string-processing problems, but will avoid any problem involving linguistic structure.

In Chapter 1 we saw strings in the abstract as sequences of symbols, which were of variable length and generally scanned in a sequential fashion, moving from one symbol to its neighbour either forwards or backwards. With strings the basic operation is matching two strings to see whether they are the same, and built upon this simple operation we have a whole host of applications.

A simple problem involving strings would be to store in the computer the names of all the current users of the computer. Perhaps we are keeping a record of how much time each person uses the computer, or perhaps we are security conscious and will only allow the people whose names we know to use the computer. Now names vary in length, and to set aside a fixed amount of storage for each name will either waste storage if we allow for long names, or lead to difficulties if we only allow a few characters per name. So the best policy would be to allow just enough storage to exactly fit each string—we shall see suitable methods later, though we have already seen these methods when discussing storage structures. An operation that we shall want to do often, is to search through all the names that we have stored, and compare them with a name that has been input, to find out whether there is a match. If we find an exact match, well and good, and we can charge this user for this period of use. If there is no match, either we have a new user, or an unauthorised user, or perhaps somebody has misspelled the name. To cope with misspellings, we could either make the unfortunate human try again, or obtain a more sophisticated matching method that will find out not only exact matches, but best matches. A second operation that we may want to do fairly often, is to add another name to the store of names so far, and also we may want to regularly delete names, when a person is no longer allowed to use our computer.

In the preceding example, with variable amounts of storage used for data, which may later be no longer required, we see all the motivation for the storage management methods of the last chapter—which management method we use, will depend upon our storage methods for strings, to be studied in detail in the next section. This example is typical of a whole set of problems, involving dictionaries and directories, tables of information where the principle information is in the form of strings.

A second class of string-processing problems are involved with **texts**. For example, the computer is used in the preparation of books. The text of the book constitutes one very long string. The important subdivisions of the string are those between sentences, paragraphs, chapters, and so on. The division into pages, and lines within the page are unimportant. Given such a text, we could use the computer to **edit** the text, searching it for particular words which are then changed, inserting new passages into the text, deleting other passages, changing the order, and so on. If we then wish to print the text, we would need to insert the page and line boundaries, number the pages: all this can be done quite mechanically, once we know the size of the line and page. This is computer typesetting. The computer can further aid the preparation of the book by scanning for keywords when preparing the index: though of course here we need some human feedback to assist the computer, for not all occurrences of a particular word will be worth indexing. Indeed, some occurrences might be blatantly incorrect: for example, the word 'bit' in a text on computing may sometimes occur in the sense 'amount', and not 'binary digit'. Also some words that we want to index might appear as grammatical variants of the word that we are searching for: for example, computer and computing. An important kind of text processor is the editor specifically designed for program texts. We shall not discuss their design specifically here, though all the components involved in their design will be covered in the following sections.

This chapter will be divided into sections in terms of techniques rather than application areas, though there is a close correspondence. We shall start by considering methods for the storage of strings, including considerations of backing store, and then go on to the matching of strings. These first two sections will have given us all the basic techniques for the first class of problems. We shall then finally discuss techniques for string manipulation, where the strings are changed by insertions or deletions or substitutions, as in the second class of problems. We shall also discuss, briefly, facets of strings peculiar to text editors.

.1 Storage methods

In considering the storage of strings, we must consider how the individual characters are stored, then how individual strings will be stored, whether by variable length vectors, or chaining, and finally we must consider how to allocate storage to collections of strings that change through time.

.1 Character codes

Strings are composed of symbols chosen from some finite alphabet. If we have n possible symbols, then we could encode the symbols or character set within a fixed quota of $\log_2 n$ bits per symbol. With 64 possible symbols, this means 6 bits, and with 128 possible symbols, 7 bits. Thus typically, computers use between 6 and 8 bits per symbol, allowing all letters, large and (possibly) small, numerals, punctuation marks, special symbols, and formating symbols. This is the situation that we shall assume for the whole of this text, with a fixed number of bits set aside for the symbols of our alphabet, without any of the complexities set out in the following paragraphs.

Complexities in character codes arise in two ways, both in the interests of efficiency. Firstly, we can recognise that some symbols will occur much more frequently than others. For example, in normal English text, the letter 'e' occurs most frequently, and the letters 'q' and 'z' only seldom, and upper-case letters are much less frequent than lower-case letters. If we use less bits for the more common symbols, and more bits for the infrequent symbols, we should on the average save! These variable length codes can indeed save appreciable storage, but have drawbacks, and are not widely used in computing. The method of Huffman for deriving the bit sequences to be

63

used for individual letters is itself very interesting, in that it uses a binary tree obtained from the probabilities of the various symbols—see exercise 3.4.1 for further references on Huffman coding.

Secondly, it may be 'natural' for the computer to work in some small number of bits, too few for the requirements of our character set. For example, we may be only allowed 6 bits per character, but want to represent both upper- and lower-case letters, 52 letters, plus other symbols which take us beyond the limit of 64 symbols in 6 bits. The answer here is to use special **shift** (or **escape**) characters, to shift from one subset of the alphabet to the other, just as on a typewriter one has shift keys to change from lower to upper case. If the shift character just acts for the character immediately following it, we obtain a variable length code of a crude kind. It is much more usual that the shift operates until it is cancelled, though of course we could include both possibilities. We could allow many different shifts to further extend our alphabet: this is often done in computer type-setting, to allow for italic, bold face, and various other scripts. By ignoring these possibilities we don't lose generality in what follows, because shift characters behave as other symbols, and we are concerned with strings as sequences of symbols, though shift characters can give extra problems, for example, when inserting a passage in italics into the middle of a text in roman script.

A final but important point about character codes is that there is usually (notably with alphanumerics) a natural ordering among the symbols: this ordering should be carried over into the encoding so that it is easy to assertain the 'less than', 'equal', 'greater than' relationships between symbols.

3.1.2 Storing single strings

We have made the assumption that the individual characters composing the string all require the same size storage slot, the same number of bits. This fixed size of storage is very convenient, and it is tempting to use the same fixed storage convention for strings. We could set aside a fixed length vector of characters, and for short strings fill out the spare room with blanks, while for strings that are too long, we just reckon too bad. This is reducing the handling of strings to the same kind of problem as handling binary encoded numbers, and avoids the whole problem of strings, their variable length. For this chapter we will ignore this fixed vector method, though I illustrate it in Fig. 3.1(*a*). However, this convention is used, and reasonably so, in most computing software such as compilers, assemblers, and operating systems—if the user supplies the computer with a name, it is either extended with blank characters to some fixed length, or truncated.

The storage of strings must take into account their variability, and we cannot assume that there is some number of characters beyond which no string will extend. We shall consider two vector methods, illustrated in Figs. 3.1(*b*) and (*c*), and four chaining methods, illustrated in Figs. 3.1(*d*) to (*g*).

The end-marker is a special symbol in our alphabet (it reduces our effective alphabet by one), and thus typically occupies 6 to 8 bits. The precount is an integer, and we must set aside enough bits for this to represent an integer in excess of the longest string that can be stored in the computer. Typically we would use between 16 and 32 bits. With vector storage, then, there is a fixed overhead per string of 6 to 8 bits for the end-marker, or 16 to 32 bits for the precount. But, we now note that the precount alternative is much more powerful—we can do everything with a precount that we can with an end-marker, and a lot more, for we know how long the string is **explicitly**. Thus when we access a string, with precount storage we will be able to access the symbols within the string at random, since we can readily check that an access remains within the string. With end-markers we have no such check, and would be constrained to sequential access only.

Thus we shall only consider the precount form of string storage. Now end-markers on strings are a natural thing for human beings, and thus **externally**, especially for input from humans, we may well use string terminators or end-markers, but **internally** will always use a precount when using vector methods.

Now consider chaining. Figs. 3.1(*d*) and (*e*), show two versions, both with a single character stored per record, but with (*d*) with one-way chaining giving us access only in one direction along the string, while the other has two way chaining to allow bidirectional movement along the string. Pointers are expensive—typically we would need 16 bits per pointer, one pointer per character, and we see that chaining of any kind is going to need some justification to make

| A | B | D | | | |

| P | Q | R | S | T | U |

(a) In a fixed length vector of six characters. Note the waste of storage, and loss of characters.

| 3 | A | B | D |

| 8 | P | Q | R | S | T | U | V | W |

(b) Variable length vector with precount.

| A | B | D | ≠ |

| P | Q | R | S | T | U | V | W | ≠ |

(c) Variable length vector with end-marker ≠.

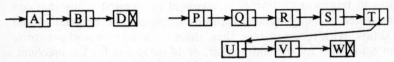

(d) One-way chained in linear list.

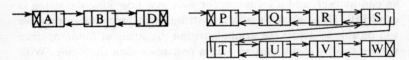

(e) Two-way chained.

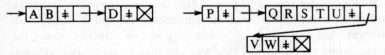

(f) Multi-character fixed record (four characters per record).

→ A B ≠ → D ≠ ⊠   → P ≠ → Q R S T U ≠ → V W ≠ ⊠

(g) Multi-character variable length record (escape pointer).

Fig. 3.1. Seven methods for storing strings. These are illustrated with two separate examples, ABD and PQRSTUVW.

the extra storage worth while. Thus we will rule out two-way chaining as completely unviable for strings, and only consider in the rest of the chapter linear lists. To further save storage, we could store many characters per record and thus reduce the relative overhead of the pointers. Two possible schemes are shown in Figs. 3.1(f) and (g).

For simplicity of exposition, we shall ignore the more complex methods of storage, though recognising that these will be very important for practical implementations. The form of the various algorithms for these storage methods will be taken up in the exercises, where practical suggestions will be found concerning problems of implementation. We shall only-consider, in the text, the vector storage with precount and linear-list methods for storing strings.

.3 Storing collections of strings

In applications, as we have seen, we shall not be simply concerned with a single string, but will be concerned with many strings. We must now consider two problems: access to the individual strings in the collection, and the allocation of storage to the strings by a storage management system.

Strings will be stored somewhere in the computer random access memory, and to access the string we will simply require an address. In our program this means a variable. For collections of strings we then require a pointer for each string, and may want to treat the collection as a unit. We could then access the collection indirectly via a vector or chain of pointers, as in Figs. 3.2(a) and (b). These two ideas are equally applicable, regardless of how the individual strings are stored. The purpose of making this point is that often strings might be stored in a two-level manner, with a pool of storage where strings are stored and a distinct piece of storage which accesses the strings. The actual methods used for the distinct accessing paths will be covered in the next chapter on tables. Which is preferable, the method of Figs. 3.2(a) or (b) or some other technique? We shall now go on to discuss the management of the storage area used for the strings using some unspecified method to access all the strings currently in the collection.

67

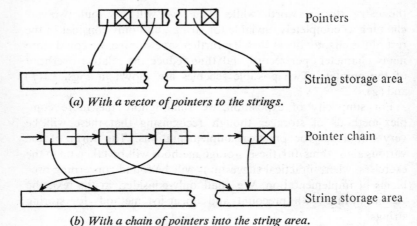

(a) With a vector of pointers to the strings.

(b) With a chain of pointers into the string area.

Fig. 3.2. Two methods for collections of strings

The strings in our collection could be stored as vectors, or linear lists. The collection could be one which is only ever added to, or it could be fixed, or it could be one that has strings both added and removed.

If the collection of strings is only ever added to, there is no

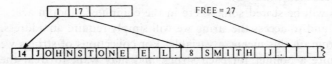

(a) The collection after two strings have been allocated.

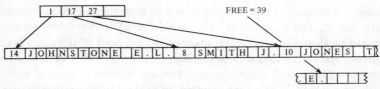

(b) The collection after the addition of a third string.

Fig. 3.3. Management of a collection of strings which is only added to. Vector storage with precount using management routines 2.1 suffices. The example shows the effect of adding a third string. Addresses are of characters, with a precount taking twice as much storage as a character.

possible advantage in using chaining, and we would use vector storage with precount, using the simple storage management set out in Routines 2.1. To see how this works on a simple example, suppose that our collection consists of persons names, and that first JOHN-STONE E. L. was inserted in storage, and then SMITH J., to give the situation of Fig. 3.3(*a*). If we assume that a precount takes twice as much storage as a character, and the addresses are for characters, this gives the addresses shown. FREE, with address value 27, points to the first position in the free area. Now consider adding JONES T. E.; this contains 10 characters, so the FREE pointer is advanced by 12 (allowing for 2 characters of storage for the precount) and the precount is set to 10, the characters inserted, and the previous value of the free pointer returned as result. This gives us the situation in Fig. 3.3(*b*).

Now if the collection is to have strings deleted from it, we require a mechanism for returning storage to the free area, and the best way for strings is via a garbage collection. Let us first of all consider vector storage, and extend the methods of the last paragraph: this leads us to the storage management methods of section 2.1.4.3 and Routines 2.5. An illustrative example is given in Fig. 3.4. Attached to every record we need extra fields for a FLAG bit, and for planning the NEXT position of the records before moving them, as shown in Fig. 3.4(*a*). The example shows the four phases of marking storage that needs to be retained (*e*), planning the moves using the NEXT field (*f*), changing the pointers in anticipation of the move (*g*) and actually making the move (*h*). In some applications the management would be slightly more complex if we use pointer fields within the records, with a recursive routine for marking the useful storage (Fig. 3.4(*e*)) and an updating scan including the pointer fields within the records (Fig. 3.4(*g*)).

For the one-way chaining method of storing strings, we will also resort to a garbage collection system, as given in section 2.1.4.2.3, Routines 2.4. It is tempting to avoid full garbage collection, but instead have a routine for returning complete strings to the free list: but this is dangerous since very often strings may have portions in common (for example, a string may be a substring of some other string). This will not be illustrated here, since storage management for chained structures of a uniform size will be illustrated in Chapter 4, Figs. 4.4 and 4.5.

COMPUTATIONAL STRUCTURES

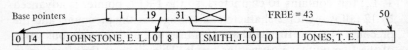

(a) *The storage record used.*

```
 1 bit   2 chars   2 chars        n chars.
        − 1 bit
┌──────┬──────────┬──────┬─────────────────┐
│ FLAG │ LENGTH n │ NEXT │     STRING      │
└──────┴──────────┴──────┴─────────────────┘
```

(b) *Three strings in storage, capacity 50 characters.*

(c) *The base pointers after the deletion of the second string: storage is at this point otherwise unaffected.*

(d) *Trying to add the string BO YCE, J. B., requiring 14 characters in the record show, fails to find enough room. Record desired is shown.*

(e) *Garbage collection is entered: firstly storage must be marked by setting the flag in all the records that can be accessed via the base pointers.*

70

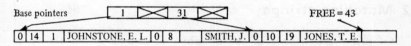

(f) *Scanning storage from record to record, using the precount to step through the records, the moves are planned using the NEXT field to store the intended location of the record after the move and at the same time all the marking FLAGs are reset.*

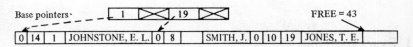

(g) *All pointers are now changed to their final values by following along the pointer to the record to which it leads, and using the NEXT field there to update this pointer: we would need to continue the process if there were any pointer within the records.*

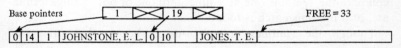

(h) *Scan the records as in (e) now shifting the records down store to fill in the deleted records.*

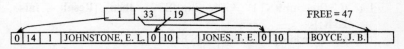

(i) *Make the addition of the new record.*

Fig. 3.4. *Management of a collection of strings which is added to and from which strings are deleted. Vector storage with precount is used, with management Routines 2.5 for full garbage collection. The example shows the effect of deleting a string, then attempting to add a string too long for the remaining free storage, which leads to garbage collection and the eventual delivery of the storage requested.*

71

3.2 Matching strings

Of prime importance in the handling of strings is the ability to compare two strings to see if they are identical, or in some way similar. This is necessary for looking up words in a dictionary, for scanning a text when forming an index, for locating a position within a text. We shall study several different forms of matching that have become widely practised: some of the methods are obvious, some require a sophisticated analysis of the problem.

3.2.1 Exact matches

The simplest kind of matching process that one can contemplate, is to test whether two strings are identical. This is the usual requirement for tables (see Chapter 4). With vector storage with precount, we only need compare the symbols within a string if they are of the same length: for one-way chaining one has no alternative but to compare the symbols one at a time until one or both strings terminate, or a first mismatch is found.

Though the routines are obvious (I hope), they are given below:

ROUTINES 3.1. *Exact matching of two strings in vector storage*
1. Match(ST1,ST2);
   ¢ strings stored in vectors with a precount ¢
   1.1. **if** Precount(ST1) $\neq$ Precount(ST2) **then** [Result $\leftarrow$ **false**; Exit;]
   1.2. $j \leftarrow 1$; **while** $j \leq$ Precount(ST1) **do**
   1.3. $_1$[**if** char(ST1,j) $\neq$ char(ST2,j) **then** [Result $\leftarrow$ **false**; Exit] $j \leftarrow j+1$;]$_1$
   1.4. **Result** $\leftarrow$ **true**; **Exit**.
2. Precount(ST);
   ¢ accesses precount LENGTH field of record ST ¢
3. Char(ST,J);
   ¢ accesses the Jth character within the string field in record ST ¢.

ROUTINES 3.2. *Exact matching of two strings in chained storage*

1. Match(ST1,ST2);

  ¢ step through the strings until either a mismatch occurs, or one
  or both of the strings terminated in a null pointer ¢

  1.1. $t1 \leftarrow$ ST1; $t2 \leftarrow$ ST2;
  1.2. **while** $t_1 \neq$ NIL **and** $t_2 \neq$ NIL **and** Char$(t_1) =$ Char(t_2) **do**
  1.3. $[t_1 \leftarrow$ Next(t_1); $t_2 \leftarrow$ Next(t_2);]
  1.4. **if** $t_1 =$ NIL **and** $t_2 =$ NIL **then** [Result $\leftarrow$ **true**;]
                    else [Result $\leftarrow$ **false**;]
  1.5. **Exit.**

2. Char(P); ¢ accesses the character field of record pointed to
   by P ¢
3. Next(P); ¢ accesses the next pointer field of record pointed to
   by P ¢

Often when matching strings we not only want to ascertain if the
strings are identical, but also wish to know if the strings do not
match, which string comes before the other in the lexicographical
ordering of the strings. Lexicographic ordering is the form of
ordering used in dictionaries and telephone directories. A simple
addition to the previous Routines 3.1 and 3.2, to check, on the first
mismatch, the ordering between the two non-identical symbols, will
give the ordering between the two strings. For strings of different
length, which match completely over the length of the shorter
string, the shorter would be taken as lower in the ordering.
Clearly in Routines 3.1, we must always match, and so step
1.1 would need to be removed and something equivalent to the
strategy of Routines 3.2 put in its place. The details are left as an
exercise.

Exact matches of strings provide basic capabilities for string
processing. The next step is to be able to scan a long string looking
for the first occurrence of a given short string, as you might do when
scanning a book looking for a particular word. This is covered in the
next section. Another line of development from string matches is
to be able to compare two strings which are not identical, and decide
if they are similar in some way. Possibilities here are briefly discussed
in section 3.2.3.

3.2.2 Substring matches

We shall now consider the very important problem of finding a particular substring within a given string. For example, starting at the beginning of the section, we may want to locate the first occurrence of the string 'particular', and would locate it in the first sentence, just over half way through. This could be a prelude to an editing action, such deleting the substring, or replacing it by something else. For the moment we just want to tackle the problem of searching a string for a substring.

The idea is straightforward: suppose that we are searching string S for substring T; then we scan S until we find the first occurrence of a match between the first symbol of T and a symbol in S, when we switch over to try to match the whole of T at this position in S. If this fails we must continue to scan along S until the next match of the first symbol of T with a symbol of S, and so on. At the first successful match we stop, returning a result to indicate where the match was found; if no match was found an error indication must be returned.

Often we do not simply wish to search for a single substring, but rather for one out of a selection of substrings. This is particularly the case where the substrings are only single symbols and occurs in, for example, assemblers, where one is searching for a field terminator which can be one of a number of possible symbols. For the general multiple substring search we require something a little different, and instead of scanning for an initial letter, and once that has been found, trying a complete match, we should try each substring in turn for a match before moving along to try again. The details should be obvious.

One application of searches for substrings is in scanning texts for the occurrences of particular words: this would be done in forming up the index of a book, or in performing an analysis upon the book, or perhaps scanning a book to find some information (in the way that one scans a book by using its index). When we specify a word for the search, there could be some ambiguity, and not all the occurrences of the word are of interest. For example, in forming the index for this book, I have an entry for the word 'record', and to form the index had to search the text for this word, but did not want all occurrences of the word, certainly wishing to ignore all uses of 'record' as a verb. To sort out these ambiguities mechanically is a fearsome task, and it makes much more sense to let the human and computer work in partnership: let the computer return all occurrences of the substring (word), and let the human select from these the ones that he wants. The retrieval of the word in context is obviously necessary if a human is to select the matches that he really wants from among those which are not relevant. This practice of searching for keywords has often been billed as 'information retrieval': I will not enter into arguments of what is or is not truly infromation retrieval, but we will see later again see keywords in an 'information retrieval' role.

.3 More complex matches

We now come to consider matches of strings in which only portions of the strings are required to match exactly, while other portions are allowed to mismatch. We will see two alternative approaches to doing this.

Let us introduce the first way through an example. Suppose that we are analysing program text, and are searching for a use of the SIN function. Then we must search for SIN followed by an opening bracket, then something, then a closing bracket, SIN(?). Of course, compilers don't work precisely in this way, but it is a general matching ability that one needs in language processing, and thus something equivalent to this is available in string-processing languages such as SNOBOL.

The '?' in the example above, SIN(?), could either be of fixed length, or of variable length, and one can represent these two cases by inventing two special symbols

* which matches any string of symbols, including the empty string,

φ which matches any single symbol.

75

Using these two special symbols, we could then match SIN(PQR) with SIN($\phi\phi\phi$) and SIN(*), but not with SIN(ϕ), and more complex matches could be made, for example using SϕN*(*) to match any of SYN(X), SINE($A+B$), SINE FUNCTION($PI*Y/B$). Clearly this kind of matching is only sensible if one of the two strings to be matched uses the special symbols * and ϕ, but not the other string. In many applications we want more than to simply know that a match is possible, and we would also like to know details of how the match was formed. That is, we would like the algorithm to return additionally pointers to where the various matches took place. In symbol manipulation languages such as SNOBOL one is allowed to insert variables into the matching string T and the variables are returned with values pointing to a position in the string S indicating where that particular point in T was matched in S.

The techniques of the last paragraph give us a form of approximate matching in which we insist on exact matches of selected substrings, but are flexible in other places. But this is not always the way we want it, and often we are willing to tolerate mismatches of symbols in any place, providing there are not too many. This is the case in spelling correction applications: for example, we may have a collection of peoples' names, and when looking up the name in the collection, not even know the correct spelling, but would hope that if we make a reasonable guess, we will find the name that we are after.

Now with spelling errors, not only will individual letters be substituted for others, but letters may be left out, or extra letters inserted. We would expect 'Tchebytchev' to be a reasonable match with 'Chebychev', and 'Smith' to be a reasonable match with 'Smyth' and even 'Smythe'. A great many techniques have been proposed, often taking into account that common errors consists of two letters in the wrong order, and other special factors. My own preferred method is based upon dynamic programming and was invented in the early 1960s by Morrison at IBM, but only recently re-invented and analysed clearly by Wagner and Fischer (*Journal A.C.M.* (January 1974)).

3.3 String manipulations

We now come to consider operations upon strings that actually alter the strings. These include simple operations such as dividing a string into two separate strings, joining two strings together to form one longer string, as well as more complex operations like deleting a few symbols from the middle of a string, and inserting a few symbols into the string. We shall consider both vector and chaining representation of the strings, and will see in general that manipulations with vector storage of strings means forming up the new string in new storage, while for the chained storage of strings all that is involved is the alteration of a few pointers.

To make the manipulations in chained storage go through cleanly, we shall slightly modify our storage: we shall precede all strings by a header record containing a void character, while pointers to strings will always point to the record immediately **preceding** the string that they indicate. This is shown in Fig. 3.5, where one pointer indicates

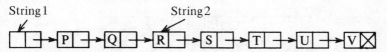

Fig. 3.5. Strings in chained storage linear list with a header record. String 1 is 'PQRSTUV' and string 2 is 'STUV'.

the complete string, while the other indicates a substring of this string. This change does affect our earlier algorithms, but not in any fundamental manner.

The manipulations to be presented will rely mainly on diagrams to communicate the techniques. The ideas are important: they are the first real exploitation of chaining with all its flexibility.

.1 Concatenation and splitting

The simplest manipulation of strings is to take one string and join it onto the end of another. For example, 'AP' joined to 'PLE' gives us 'APPLE'. This operation is known as *concatenation*, and very often is symbolised by an infix operator '+'. Thus we have the equation 'AP'+'PLE' = 'APPLE'.

In vector storage we would have to form the concatenation so that all the symbols are contiguous in storage: but in general the component strings will be stored at very different parts of storage, and could not be joined up as they are. The solution is to form up the concatenation in a new record whose length is the sum of the two component records. This is schematised in Fig. 3.6(*a*).

In chained storage for strings the symbols are not necessarily contiguous, and it is the pointers which indicate the sequence of the symbols within a string. Thus it is very possible to concatenate two strings by changing the value of a pointer. Consider Fig. 3.6(*b*). Initially the end of string *S* is marked by a null pointer in the third record: to add something to the end of *S* we simply overwrite this null pointer with a pointer which leads to the next symbol in the desired sequence. The effect of concatenating *S* and *T* is shown in the second diagram. The result occupies the same storage as the original strings, and *S* has been altered also!!

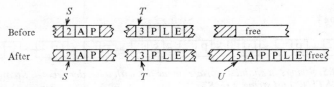

(*a*) *Vector storage.*

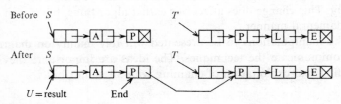

(*b*) *Chained storage.*

Fig. 3.6. *Concatenation of string S* = '*AP*' *to string T* = '*PLE*' *to form U* = *Concatenate* (*S,T*), *i.e.* '*APPLE*'.

Now let us consider the converse operation: given a string, let us split it into two at some specified point. This point within the string could have been found by a previous search process for a substring, or be some fixed number of characters into the string. A position within a string is very easily indicated in the chained storage representation: it is simply a pointer into the string, to some record down the chain (as in Fig. 3.5). A position within a string in vector storage must be specified by the string (a pointer to the record) and the position within the string (an integer).

The results of splitting a string in vector storage is shown in Fig. 3.7(*a*). The two new strings are formed in new storage, leaving the original string intact.

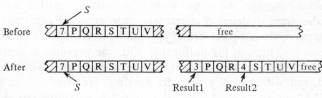

(a) Vector storage.

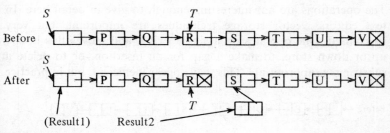

(b) Chained storage.

Fig. 3.7. Splitting string 'PQRSTUV' into 'PQR' and 'STUV'.

The results of splitting a string in chained storage is shown in Fig. 3.7(*b*): the point for splitting is indicated by *T* (note that this points to record just before the second string) and the two results are formed using the original records plus one extra for the header record of the second string. Note that while the actual pointer values of *S* and *T* have not been changed, the strings to which they lead are now both changed.

At this stage the reason for the change in our convention for chained storage of strings should be abundantly apparent: changing a string meant changing pointers, usually just before a character within the string that has been selected.

79

3.3.2 Deletions and insertions

We now consider how to effect more elaborate changes to strings, to delete portions of a string, and to insert a string into another string. These are essential manipulations for text editing, but are of importance in other applications.

In vector storage, we would start at a position i within string S, and either have to delete N characters, or insert some other string T. For deletion, the simplest strategy would be to change the N characters to voids, though for uniformity with the previous actions, the sensible thing to do would be to form up a new string within a new record, but with the N characters missing. We would need to be careful about error conditions, that our deleted characters do not extend beyond the end of the string. Similarly, to insert the string T at that point, we would form a new record with the new string in it. The operations are not interesting enough to give in detail here. In text editors, vector storage techniques are important, but very specialised. One operates on a single string, and moves this bodily up or down store, to make a gap for an insertion, or to delete a substring, as appropriate. This may appear inefficient, but in practice

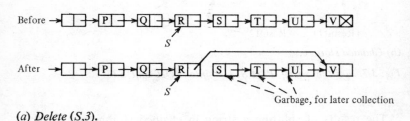

(a) *Delete (S,3)*.

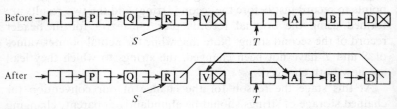

(b) *Insert (S,T)*.

Fig. 3.8. Deletion and insertion with chained storage of strings.

either the computer is dedicated to this single task, or it is shared and only small strings are involved in the shifts (see Exercise 3.4.10).

In chained storage we would start with a position within a string indicated by a pointer S, and either delete N symbols from this point on, or insert some other string T. Fig. 3.8(a) shows what happens on deleting 3 characters from the middle of a string (the deleted records would later be added to the free list during a garbage collection), while Fig. 3.8(b) shows what happens when a string is added into the middle of a string. Note that the original string pointers still have the same values, but that side-effects have altered the strings they lead to.

ROUTINES 3.3. *Deleting and inserting with chained storage of strings*
1. Delete(S,N);
   ¢ delete N symbols form string at position S ¢
   1.1. ¢ step on N symbols checking for end ¢
   $$i \leftarrow 0; \text{temp} \leftarrow S;$$
   while $i \leq N$ **and** temp $\neq$ NIL **do** [$i \leftarrow i+1$; temp $\leftarrow$ Next(temp);]
   1.2. ¢ effect deletion by updating pointers ¢
   Setnext(S,temp); **Exit.**
2. Insert(S,T);
   ¢ insert string T into another string at point S ¢
   ¢ must allow that either S or T or both are empty ₵
   2.1. ¢ scan to last record of T ¢
   temp $\leftarrow T$; **while** Next (temp) $\neq$ NIL **do** [temp $\leftarrow$ Next (temp);]
   2.2. ¢ insert lower part of S at end of T ¢
   Set next (temp, Next (S));
   2.3. ¢ insert T at end of upper part of S ¢
   Set next(S,Next(T));
   2.4. **Exit.**

.4 Exercises

.1 Write a routine for translating strings (in vector storage) to and from the usual fixed size character codes and a variable length Huffman code. Design the particular code yourself, with the aid of suitable computer programs of course, so that the storage saving is as large as possible. For information about Huffman codes, see either Huffman, D. A., *Proc. I.R.E.*, vol. 4D, no. 9, pp. 1098–101, or Wells, M., *Computer Journal*, vol. 15, no. 4, pp. 308–13. The first of these deals with the basic method of Huffman coding, while the second applies Huffman coding to the saving of storage in program files.

3.4.2 Write a routine which makes a match using the special symbols ϕ and *, returning as answers pointers to both ends of all the * matched portions.

3.4.3 Program the algorithm which measures the difference between two strings using dynamic programming, as described by Wagner and Fischer (*Journal A.C.M.* (January 1974)).

3.4.4 Extend the dynamic programming method for approximate string matching so that it will search a string for a substring match to within a preset tolerance d.

3.4.5 Write a complete string processing system. Use simple linear lists for the storage of the strings (as Fig. 3.1(d)) with a header record (as Fig. 3.5) to aid the manipulations. Implement the system in three phases, as set out below:

Phase 1. This is the machine- and language-dependent part of the implementation. You want records of three fields, FLAG, CHARACTER, and POINTER, and how you program these depends upon the size of your computer machine word, and upon the way characters are handled within your programming system. If your machine word is 24 bits, 32 bits, or longer, you would pack all three fields into a single word, while for 16 bits and 12 bit machines you would use 2 words of storage. Having decided a policy for the storage of records and the fields within them, set aside an area of storage for all the records you will need (it is a good idea to make this easily adjustable, testing your program with a small area, and later enlarging it for the application of your string manipulation program). Now write routines for accessing and updating the fields within a record referred to by its address or subscript (if in a high-level language).

You will require routines Flag(P), Setflag(P,V), Character(P), Setcharacter(P,V), Pointer(P), Setpointer(P,V) which either access the named field in record pointed to by P, or update the field to value V. You may find it easier to program using an auxiliary routine Pack(P,F,C,Q) which packs into the record pointed to by P all three field values F, C, and Q. Then setting values into the fields could be done using the field access routines and Pack. Note that the FLAG field is only used by the storage management routines of Phase 2, being set and reset during garbage collection: thus you could treat this field specially, ignoring it or always setting it to **false** (bit value 0) during the routines which operate on the other two fields.

In all your routines test to see that the arguments are within a legitimate range, and print an error message if they are not, and then assume some default value before continuing with the program execution. This is particularly important for the pointer arguments, to protect against accessing a record which is not there (especially the null pointer). You will appreciate this refinement when you come to later stages of this program implementation.

Routines for inputting and outputting characters, and for comparing two characters, are also usually machine dependent (this is especially true of Algol-60 and Fortran) and so it is also a good idea to write suitable routines at this stage.

Test these routines thoroughly, both separately and together, testing also all the error conditions, so that when proceeding to Phase 2 you have complete faith in the correctness of these Phase 1 routines.

Phase 2. From Phase 1 you have the ability to handle records: from now on you never access storage directly, but only indirectly via pointers to records. In this phase you arrange the management of these records into strings. You will need all the routines of a full storage management system, as set out in Routines 2.4 using the POINTER field here as the NEXT field of the management system. You will also need an input routine for complete strings, and an output routine (take care to add the header record on input, and not to print it on output). Also write a routine for making copies of strings (this will be very similar to your input routine).

Test these chained storage routines very thoroughly. To assist your testing, write a routine which dumps the whole of the record storage area with the values of the three fields (thus test the routines with only a small number of records). Use this dump routine frequently to ensure that all operations are using the chaining in the way that you expect. In the dump routine also print out all the standard pointers, NIL, FREE, and the base pointers that preserve strings through garbage collection.

Phase 3. String manipulation. From Phase 2 you have the ability to input and output strings, and to make copies of them, while from Phase 1 you have the ability to access and update the fields within records.

You are now all set up to program the routines of section 3.3. In addition to the routines for splitting and concatenating, deleting and inserting, you will also find useful an auxiliary routine Step(P,N) for stepping the pointer P on N characters along the string, as well as a Routine for searching for a substring as in Section 3.2.2. In all routines you must take great care of error conditions, in particular to avoid moving beyond the end of a string.

Again you must thoroughly test these routines, using a small amount of storage and dumping it in order to ascertain that exactly what you expected does in fact happen. Again you must also test error circumstances such a searching for a nonexistent substring, as well as the normal operation of the routines.

Phase 4. You now have a correctly working string processing system, and have in effect extended the programming language that you started with to include strings and string processing. You now can use it to edit your programs, changing round the order in which you did things, and so on. You could also investigate your programming style, to see how often you use particular statements, comparing the score with those of other peoples programs. As a more difficult application of your string-processing system, you could try your hand at symbolic differentiation—read in algebraic expression as a string in the conventions of normal programming languages, and differentiate this with respect to one of the variables. You will find recursion very handy here.

4.6 Extend the programming project of Exercise 3.4.5 to include gap matching with variables as in Exercise 3.4.2. Does this materially help you in solving the formal differentiation problem?

4.7 Set up a string-processing system as in Exercise 3.4.5, only using a different method of string storage.

For chained storage with many characters per record, you will need to use void characters to fill out records to the right length, and for deletions fill out with voids. Then during garbage collection you will need an extra phase to shift characters in order to remove voids from the middle of strings. Note that there are severe difficulties with pointers into the middle of strings if these are to survive garbage collection.

4.8 Program an interactive internal text editor along the lines of section 3.3.3. This means inventing a command language for the interaction: say a single letter operation to indicate movement of the editing pointer, searching, deletion, insertion, together with one operand, either a string or an integer. If you can find any commercial interactive text editors, study their commands carefully and do not hesitate to learn from their ideas.

4.9 As Exercise 3.4.8, but for insertions and deletions use an 'escape pointer' convention as in Fig. 3.1(g). You will need to program a garbage collection routine to recover the storage that becomes lost in pointers: the easiest way to do this is to output the string onto some external storage such as magnetic tape or discs, losing the pointers on the way, and then read it back in.

.10 Program an external editor on discs. For storage on discs, use fixed size storage records containing two pointers, one to the next record of text, and one to the previous record of text. The amount of text per record will depend largely upon the characteristics of the disc available, and would be coupled to the formatting of the disc. The string as stored on the disc is then a two-way chained sequence of records, and we can insert and delete from this chain simply by changing pointers. To manage the records on disc we would need to maintain a 'map' of the disc internally, so that at any moment we know precisely what portions of the disc available to us are free for us to write to.

How much text we keep internally depends upon how much primary storage we have: we could get away with a single record, though might find it convenient to have several records internally at once. As we move our pointer forwards or backwards we will need to follow the disc chaining inputting and outputting records appropriately. Deleting and inserting change the contents of the disc records, and eventually as the changes become substantial, the actual disc chaining will be affected. At the end of editing we would in general end with a partially filled record in the middle of the text: to avoid leaving voids in the middle, we would then need to scan the string to the end, this having the effect of shifting the string down through the records, possibly freeing a record at the end.

Note that if a text editor like this is to be released for use within a disc-operating system, all file conventions would need changing to include the convention used here: at the very least this means extending all the file-handling routines to handle files in this format (they often already include the ability to handle more than one kind of format). Of course you might strike it lucky, and existing sequential files could be exploited for this kind of editor.

4 Files and tables

We will call any collection of data that is thought of as a unit, a **file**. Examples of files are: the details of all the employees in a business; a program; all the programs belonging to a group of people; the collection of measurements made during a scientific experiment.

There are five basic operations on files, falling into two subsets. These are:

File maintenance
  (i) Inserting a new item into the file.
 (ii) Updating (changing) an existing item in the file.
(iii) Deleting one or more items from the file.

Report writing
 (iv) Retrieving an individual item from the file.
  (v) Retrieving global information from the file, such as statistics, or the printing out of the entire file.

There is an additional facet of files with which we will not be too concerned here. This is **file creation**, in which the area of storage for the file is prepared for it, the storage area required set aside, identified as reserved for this file, and so on. For large files we would also need the capability of starting them off with an initial set of data during a **bulk-load** of the file. This may require special techniques which will not be explored in this book.

Commonly a collection of files which are related (for example, they may all be used by a single company within its business) are called a **data-base**. The treatment of data-bases within an integrated framework is called data-base management. A proper treatment of this important subject is beyond the scope of this book, though we will see some facets of it in section 4.3.

87

The units of data of which the file is composed we shall call **data records** or simply **records**. It is hoped that this will not lead to terminological confusion between storage records and data records: which is intended should be clear from context. Within records there are further subdivisions, called (naturally) **fields,** and these could be further subdivided into subfields, and so on. Similarly we could divide the file into subunits, larger than a single record, calling these units **subfiles.** Fig. 4.1 illustrates the structure of a file which contains

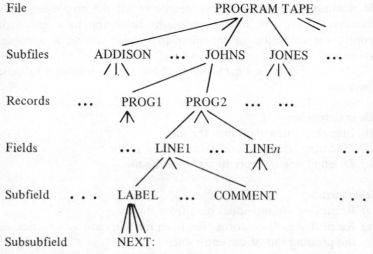

Fig. 4.1. A hierarchical file structure: the file contains the programs of many individual people as a tree.

the programs of many different people. The individual programs are the records, and the programs belonging to a single person comprise the subfiles. Within the records there would be fields comprising the lines or statements of the program, and these might be further divided into subfields of labels, operation codes, and so on. Of course we could have called the lines of program the records: it is partly a matter of preference. Through this example we see that a file very naturally acquires a hierarchical tree structure.

The hierarchical structure of the file also reflects the paths of access for processing of individual items in the file. To remind you, we had said that one node of a graph was **directly accessible** from a second node if there was a directed (or undirected) edge from the second node to the first, while it was **accessible** if there was a sequence of edges, a path, from the second to the first. Clearly in processes which act on a single item of data, we would select the file, then the subfile, then the subsubfile, and so on until the item, be it record, field, or subfile, has been located. For global processing of the entire file, such as printing it out, information at all levels of the file would be required, and we would need to traverse the entire file, in effect performing a generalised pre-order tree traversal.

Now, while the hierarchical structure reflects the 'natural' structure of the file, the actual structure in the storage medium may be very different. Sometimes this different structure will be imposed by the storage medium, and sometimes by special processing requirements. Any structure which contains at least the same access paths as the original hierarchical description of the file will be usable, even though the direct accesses may be radically different. In analysing a file structure we shall use the path length from tree root to the item of interest as a measure of time taken to find the required item, usually averaging over all items in the file, and over all possible selections of items for the file, in order to ascertain the efficiency of that file storage structure.

The simplest form of file would have no subfiles, and consist purely of records with two fields of significance, which we shall call the key and the entry. The key is the part of the record by which the record is identified, while the entry contains the information that will be required during report writing. We shall call such a file a **table**.

For storage between times of processing, files require storing on some **external medium** which could be **physical**, such as punched cards or punched paper tape, or which could be **magnetic**, such as magnetic tapes or discs, or occasionally it might be optical or some other exotic medium. All forms of storage external to the computer are known as **backing store** (though some readers may find this term applied to physical storage media a bit novel).

During the processing of a file it can happen that the file is sufficiently small to fit entirely within the random access core memory of the computer—in this case we shall say that it is **internal**. Also it often does happen that the whole life of the file, especially for tables, is internal: it is generated internally during the execution

89

of some larger process and is used temporarily during that process (for example, assembler symbol tables).

The central problem of this chapter is how shall we organise our files and tables so that the operations on the file can be as efficiently executed as possible? We shall see a variety of techniques, starting with internal tables, then external files, and finally complex files requiring many different paths of access, where the structure is that of a graph rather than a tree.

4.1 Internal tables

We now take up the detailed study of tables stored internally. Such tables are of most importance in assemblers and compilers (as symbol tables) but will also occur frequently in other applications.

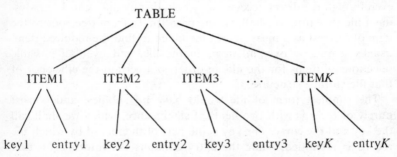

Fig. 4.2. The hierarchical structure of a table.

We have seen how, in Chapter 2, random access core storage can be structured in any way that is desired. Thus for internal tables we will be able to structure the table in any way that suits our purpose. The way that we structure our table will critically influence the efficiency with which the various operations on the table can be achieved. Speed of operation is important, but not necessarily of paramount importance. Also important is storage requirements, and programming effort. Programming effort is a very important consideration, and we shall be concerned with trade-offs between speed and storage requirements, and programming effort.

We shall study seven rival methods for the storage and manipulation of tables, analysing these under three general headings which broadly describe the kind of structure being used. We have seen that a table is a primitive form of file, with a hierarchical tree structure as in Fig. 4.2. The edges of the tree represent the access paths required, **but these access paths need not be direct.** The first general class of techniques uses a sequential access strategy, while the second makes the tree more extensive, and only the third class of techniques makes the paths of access direct or almost direct.

Operations on the tables are always made with respect to the key, and perform actions involving the entry. The operations, the same as those given in general terms earlier, are:

(i) Insertion: given a (key,entry) pair, insert the entry into the table so that it may later be located using the key.

(ii) Update: given a (key,entry) pair, locate the item with the given key and change its entry to the value specified.

(iii) Deletion: given a key, delete the complete item, key and entry, from the table.

(iv) Look-up: given a key, find the corresponding entry.

(v) Printout: list all the (key,entry) pairs of the table. We shall always consider that this should be in sorted order, as determined by the keys. Not all applications require a table printout (for example, it is not usual for the symbol table of compilers to be printed out, though it is usual for the symbol table of an assembler to be printed out). For table printout we shall only consider table methods where the table is maintained in sorted order, though there is always the alternative of maintaining the table unsorted, and then sorting the items just prior to printout.

Note that all the insertion routines that we give will assume that given key does not already appear in the table, or if it does, a second record with the same key is required. The update routine provides the means for changing the entry of an already existing record. We may very often need to combine these two routines into a single insertion/update routine which updates the entry if an item already exists with the given key, otherwise inserts a new item into the table. The deletion routines also assume that only one item with the specified key exists (or none, in which case an error condition results): if more than one item with the specified key exists, only one is deleted: the reader is invited to generalise the routines given to cater for this more general deletion requirement.

For analysis of efficiency, we shall always denote by K the number of items in the table, and by N the total number of storage slots required. In general there will be three kinds of storage slot required, for the key, the entry, and for pointers in methods that use chaining. Typically the slot for the entry will be largest, then the slot for the key, with pointers being smallest. This aspect is discussed again in section 4.1.4.

To illustrate the methods, we will use a standard example, with strings as keys and entries, as in Table 4.1.

Order of arrival	Key	Entry
1	MOV	Birmingham
2	CMP	London
3	BJY	Plymouth
4	BIC	Carlow
5	BJH	Herts
6	AXN	London
7	UHW	Bristol
8	JSR	Angus
9	BER	Cambs
10	JMP	London

Table 4.1. The standard example to be used for illustrating table technique. The data shows the conversion from motor-car number codes in Britain, to the county or town that uses that code. Thus all cars that have 'MOV' as part of their registration number, come from Birmingham. The data is shown in order of arrival for the formation of the table.

4.1.1 Sequential tables

These are the very simplest forms of table, and the ones that would be used for small tables, and for tables where the speed of operations is not important. The table is structured so that the rule of access is **serial** or **sequential**, starting at one end and stepping through from there to the other end. Looking only at direct accesses, this makes the table into a linear tree (hence this method for tables is often known as **linear**)—but the basic hierarchical structure is still maintained through sequences of direct accesses. This is shown in Fig. 4.3(a). The indirect paths of access are shown by broken lines,

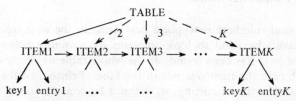

(a) Structure. Full lines give direct access paths, while broken lines show indirect access—these are weighted to show the number of direct accesses required.

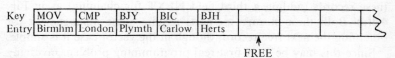

(b) Example in vector storage, 5 items unsorted.

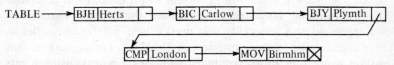

(c) Example in chained storage, 5 items unsorted. Storage records have three fields, named KEY, ENTRY, and NEXT respectively.

Fig. 4.3. *Sequential access table.*

weighted by the number of direct accesses involved. Clearly for a random item which is in the table, we would have to, on the average, travel halfway to locate an item (locating an item means comparing keys until a match has been found), and thus on the average there are approximately $K/2$ comparisons of keys and accesses to storage. The exact figures will depend upon the particular storage technique that we are using.

The linear tree on which the table is based can be stored either using vector storage, or using chained storage. Figs. 4.3(b) and (c) show these for the example of Table 4.1. In addition to the alternative methods of storage, there is the possibility of maintaining the sequence of items in sorted order, being sorted by key. Thus altogether four variations arise, which will be considered in the next two sections, first unsorted tables, and then sorted tables.

4.1.1.1 Unsorted sequential tables

The general rule here is to place new items in the next free storage record available, and to look-up items by scanning either until a match of keys has been found, or the whole table has been scanned, in which case the item was not in the table. Printout of the table is not possible without sorting, so will not be considered.

To store the items in the table we need records of storage with (at least) two fields KEY and ENTRY. The whole table can be stored either using a vector of these records, as in Fig. 4.3(b), or a chain of these records (adding a third field NEXT for chaining) as in Fig. 4.3(c). Both these storage methods require some management for obtaining the next free record, though in the vector case it is simple.

Since this may be your first real programming problem involving records and chaining, it is worth considering an example in some detail. Details will differ from problem to problem, from computer (or programming language) to computer: the routines that follow are expressed at a generality that masks these differences, so let us here examine the example problem of Table 4.1. Let us imagine that we are using a fictitious computer with 24-bit words, using 8 bits per character, and thus storing 3 characters per word. Words are directly addressable, but not characters. The key then fits conveniently into a single word, as does a pointer, while entries will require two words of storage. Now consider how the example tables of Fig. 4.3 are stored. Fig. 4.4 shows these tables in an area of storage with base address STORE, with pointers being offsets from this base. Fig. 4.4(a) shows the vector storage example of Fig. 4.3(b), while Fig. 4.4(b) shows the example of Fig. 4.3(c) and Fig. 4.4(c) shows a more complex situation which appears later as Fig. 4.5(b). Also shown on the figure are the field accessing routines: keys and pointers are handed to and from the routines by value, while entries being larger than a single word are handed to and from the routines by 'reference', the address in storage as the offset relative to base STORE.

The routines for the five operations to be considered are very similar for both storage methods, with the exception of deletions—for vector storage deletions is simple, while for chaining it is quite

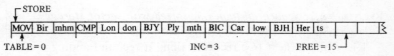

⌐STORE																	
MOV	Bir	mhm	CMP	Lon	don	BJY	Ply	mth	BIC	Car	low	BJH	Her	ts			

TABLE = 0   INC = 3   FREE = 15

(a) Example of Fig. 4.3(b) in vector storage.

NIL = −1

⌐STORE															
MOV	Bir	mhm	−1	CMP	Lon	don	0	BJY	Ply	mth	4	BIC	Car	low	8
BJH	Her	ts	12				24				28				32

TABLE = 16   FREE = 20

(b) Example of Fig. 4.3(c) in chained storage.

NIL = −1   FREE = 8   TABLE = 28

⌐STORE															
MOV	Bir	mhm	−1	CMP	Lon	don	0	BJY	Ply	mth	32	BIC	Car	low	4
BJH	Her	ts	12	AXN	Lon	don	16	UHW	Bri	stl	20	JSR	Ang	us	24
			36				40				44				

(c) Example of Fig. 4.5(b) in chained storage.

Fig. 4.4. Sequential tables, unsorted, showing an example with storage allocated to the items. The problem is as in Table 4.1, with a fictitious 24-bit (addressable) word computer and 8-bit character code: thus a key fits in 1 word, an entry in 2 words, and a pointer in 1 word.

Field accessing and updating routines are:

Key(R); Result ← STORE [R] ¢ contents of location R within STORE ¢;
Entry(R); Result ← $R+1$ ¢ reference to entry within STORE ¢;
Next(R); Result ← STORE [$R+3$] ¢ contents of location R+3 within STORE ¢;
Setkey(R,K); STORE[R] ← K;
Setentry(R,E); STORE[$R+1$] ← STORE[E]; STORE[$R+2$] ← STORE[$E+1$];
Setnext (R,P); STORE[$R+3$] ← P;

complex. The routines will be presented in a way that makes the similarities stand out, commenting the routines identically where possible.

We shall see later that there is no advantage in the unsorted chained sequential table—but I have included it as a simple example of chaining, and for anyone unfamiliar with chaining a detailed study of these routines is encouraged.

ROUTINES 4.1. *Sequential tables, unsorted with vector storage*
1. Insert(K,E); ¢ insert item (K,E) into table TABLE ¢
    1.1. ¢ obtain next free record, calling it rec, and adding it to the table ¢
        if FREE $> N$ ¢ storage limit ¢
        then [¢ no more storage: error ¢ **Exit**;]
        else [rec ← FREE; FREE ← FREE+INC;]
    1.2. ¢ insert values into fields of record ¢
        Setkey(rec,K); Setentry(rec,E);
    1.3. **Exit**.
2. Update(K,E); ¢ update the entry field of record K to value E ¢
    2.1. ¢ start with rec pointing to start of table ¢
        rec ← TABLE;
    2.2. **while** ¢ more records ¢ rec $<$ FREE **do**
    2.3. $_1$[**if** ¢ K indicates this record ¢ $K =$ Key(rec)
    2.4.   **then**$_2$[¢ update and exit ¢ Setentry(rec,E); **Exit**]$_2$
    2.5.   **else**$_3$[¢ continue to next record in sequence ¢
              rec ← rec+INC;]$_3$
        ]$_1$
    2.6. ¢ error—item not in table ¢ **Exit**.
3. Delete(K); ¢ delete from table item with key K ¢
    3.1 to 3.3. as Update
    3.4.   **then**$_2$[¢ swap with end record and free the record ¢
             FREE ← FREE−INC;
             Setkey(rec,Key(FREE)); Setentry(rec,Entry (FREE));
             Exit.]$_2$
    3.5 and 3.6. as Update.
4. Look-up(K); ¢ look-up the entry corresponding to key K ¢
    4.1 to 4.3. as Update
    4.4. **then**$_2$[¢ return entry as result ¢
        Result ← Entry(rec); **Exit**;]$_2$
    4.5 and 4.6. as Update.
¢ Auxiliary routines ¢

5. Initialise; ¢ initialises table and free area ¢
    5.1. FREE ← 0; INC ← ¢ size of record ¢; TABLE ← 0; **Exit.**
6. Key(R); Entry(R); Setkey(R,K); Setentry(R,E);
    ¢ these access and update the fields of record R ¢

ROUTINES 4.2. *Sequential tables, unsorted with chained storage*
1. Insert(K,E); ¢ insert item (K,E) into table TABLE ¢
    1.1. ¢ obtain next free record, calling it rec, add to table ¢
        if FREE = NIL **then**[¢ no more storage: error ¢ **Exit;**]
            else₁[rec ← FREE; FREE ← Next(FREE);
                Setnext(rec,TABLE); TABLE ← rec;]₁
    1.2. ¢ insert values into fields of record ¢
        Setkey(rec,K); Setentry(rec,E);
    1.3. **Exit.**
2. Update(K,E); ¢ update the entry field of record K to value E ¢
    2.1. ¢ start with rec pointing to start of table ¢
        rec ← TABLE;
    2.2. **while** ¢ more records ¢ rec ≠ NIL **do**
    2.3.   ₁[**if** ¢ K indicates this record ¢ K = Key(rec)
    2.4.   **then**₂[¢ update and exit ¢ Setentry(rec,E); **Exit.**]₂
    2.5.   **else**₃[¢ continue to next record in sequence ¢
                rec ← Next(rec);]₃
        ]₁
    2.6. ¢ error—item not in table ¢ **Exit.**
3. Delete(K); ¢ delete from table item with key K ¢
    3.1.   **if** ¢ table not empty ¢ TABLE ≠ NIL **then**
    3.2.   ₁[¢ start to search at beginning of table ¢
        rec ← TABLE;
    3.3.   **if** ¢ first record is the one ¢ K = Key(TABLE)
    3.4.   **then**₂[¢ delete this record from the table ¢
                TABLE ← Next(TABLE);
    3.5.   ¢ return record to free list ¢
                Setnext(rec,FREE); FREE ← rec;
                Exit,]₂
    3.6.   **else**₃[¢ search remaining table ¢
            while ¢ more records ¢ Next(rec) ≠ NIL **do**
    3.7.   ₄[**if** ¢ next record the one ¢ K = Key(Next(rec))
    3.8.   **then**₅[¢ delete next record from table ¢
                temp ← Next(rec);

97

                  Setnext(rec,Next(temp));

3.9.   ¢ return record to free list ¢

                  Setnext(temp,FREE); FREE ← temp;$]_5$

3.10.   **else**$_6$[¢ continue to next record ¢

            rec ← Next(rec);$]_6$

           $]_4$

         $]_3$

       $]_1$

3.11. ¢ error—item not in table ¢ **Exit**.

4. Lookup(K); ¢ look-up entry corresponding to key K ¢

    4.1, 4.2, and 4.3. as Update.

    4.4.   **then**$_2$[¢ return entry as result ¢

              Result ← Entry(rec); **Exit**.$]_2$

    4.5 and 4.6. as Update.

¢ Auxiliary routines ¢

5. Initialise; ¢ initialises table and free area ¢

    5.1. NIL ← −1; TABLE ← NIL; FREE ← 0;

    5.2. N ← ¢ size limit of table ¢; INC ← ¢ size of record ¢;

    5.3. i ← 0; **while** $i < N$ **do** [Setnext(i,i+INC); $i ← i +$ INC;];

    5.4. Setnext(N,NIL);

    5.5. **Exit**.

6. Key(R); Entry(R); Next(R); Setkey(R,K); Setentry(R,E); Setnext(R,P); ¢ these access and update the fields in record R. It is these routines that contain the assumptions of record size. ¢

The vector storage routines should be clear, after reference to Fig. 4.3(b). Note that we could have factored out an auxiliary routine Next which added INC to the pointers, thus making the superficial similarity between the two storage methods even greater. As they stand, all storage management is included within the routines (apart from initialise), and in the chained storage algorithm there is a case for using a constructor routine, even though this would only be used in one place within the insert routine. Note that if we did not have a requirement for deletions, the storage management aspect for chaining could be much simpler: we do not need a free list, but could simply maintain a pointer FREE in a manner identical to the method used for the vector storage routines.

It is worth discussing how the chained storage routines work. Fig. 4.5(a) shows an example with 8 items in the table: the sequence

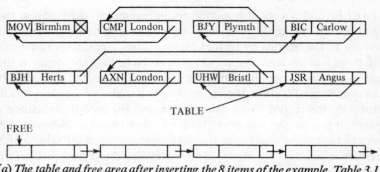

(a) The table and free area after inserting the 8 items of the example, Table 3.1.

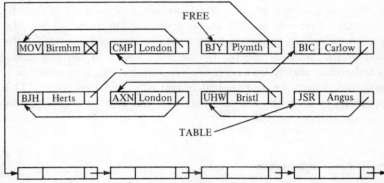

(b) The table and free area after the deletion of the record with key BIT.

Fig. 4.5. The action of deleting a record in a chained sequential table.

of items in the table start at position TABLE, record 8 if we number the records from 1 from the top left. MOV was the first item inserted, then CMP, then BJY, and so on, and thus MOV is in record 1, CMP in record 2, BJY in record 3, and the chaining within the table is physically backwards from record 8 to record 1. Logically the actual positions of the records is unimportant, this being taken care of in the chaining. The free-list starts with record 9 and then chains forwards up to the limit of storage. If we were to add a 9-th item to the table, it would be placed in record 9, and the free list pointer FREE advanced along its chain to record 10. Now let us consider what happens when we delete a record. Let us delete the record whose key is BJY. In outline, we must scan the table, starting at

99

TABLE, and locate the record to be removed, then adjust the pointers in the table to bypass record 3, and finally return this record to the free-list by further modification of pointers. The result of these actions is shown in Fig. 4.5(*b*). Note that the items in the table are no longer in contiguous storage slots, but that that is unimportant. To effect the changes to the table, we need to locate not only the record to be deleted, but also the record immediately preceding it in the sequence. Had we used two-way chaining this would have been easy: with one-way chaining we must take as our reference point as we move down the chain, the record just before the record whose key we inspect. It is this that makes the deletion routine more complex than the lookup and update routines.

The routines can all be made more efficient by using a dummy terminating record: initially this is given the key searched for, and then since we can guarantee to find the key, we need not test for the end of the table during the search, but simply at the end check whether the search was successful or not by checking whether it terminated with the dummy end record or some other record. This is easiest to do with vector storage, but can also be done with the chained storage version.

4.1.1.2 Sorted sequential tables

In the previous section the methods used did not permit us to print-out the table sorted by key. We could of course printout the table in the random order in which they arrived: for chained storage this means the last to arrive is printed first, while for vector storage the order could either be last arrived first printed or first arrived first printed. Deletions would upset these orders. An alternative would be to sort the items into the correct order just before printout: methods for this will be explored in detail in Chapter 5. Here we will consider maintaining the record sequences in sorted order, so that the table is always ready for printout. We will see in Chapter 5 that sorted table methods give us one class of sorting techniques!

To maintain the table in sorted order, we must change the way we inserted the new item into the table, not placing the item where it is most convenient, but rather searching the table for the correct position. The deletion method for vector storage is then severely altered in order to maintain the ordering after removal of the item, while the look-up and update can exploit the ordering so as to avoid scanning the complete table for an item that is not there. The routines for the two candidate storage methods now become fairly different, though the basic searching methods are still, of course, the same.

For vector storage, when we insert a new item, we must shift items up storage to make room for the new item at its correct place, while on deletion we must move items down store to close up the gap left by the deleted item. This makes the routines really very similar to the routines for insertion and deletion of strings in vector storage, studied in Chapter 3. The insertion technique that we will use is by **bubbling** a new item in from the top end of the table: we compare the new key with topmost key, and if the result shows that the new key is greater, we insert at the end, otherwise we shift the topmost record up one place, and compare the new key with the second topmost item, and so on until we either have found the point of insertion or have reached the bottom of the table. This bubbling idea is also frequently known as **sifting**, and sometimes as shuttling, and will be used again in sorting. For deletion a bubbling method is not appropriate, and the routine first locates the item to be deleted, then moves records down to close the gap.

ROUTINES 4.3. *Sequential tables, sorted, with vector storage*
1. Insert(K,E); ¢ bubble insertion of item (K,E) into the correctly ordered position in the table ¢
   1.1. ¢ make room for new item and prepare for scan ¢
      if FREE $>$ N—INC ¢ limit of storage ¢
      then [¢ no more storage: error ¢ **Exit**;]
      else [rec $\leftarrow$ FREE$-$INC; FREE $\leftarrow$ FREE$+$INC;]
   1.2. **while** ¢ position not found ¢ rec $\geq$ TABLE **and** $K <$ Key(rec) **do**
   1.3. $_1$[¢ shift record up one place ¢ next $\leftarrow$ rec$+$INC; Setkey(next,Key(rec)); Setentry(next,Key(rec));
   1.4. ¢ move down one record ¢
      rec $\leftarrow$ rec$-$INC;]$_1$
   1.5. ¢ insert item (K,E) at this point ¢ rec $\leftarrow$ rec$+$INC; Setkey(rec ,K); Setentry(rec ,K);
   1.6. **Exit**.

101

The remaining routines are similar either to the above, or to the unsorted routines, and are left as an exercise.

For chained storage, to make the insertion we must scan the table to find the correct place of insertion, and then effect the insertion by the suitable adjustment of pointers. We need to take special action

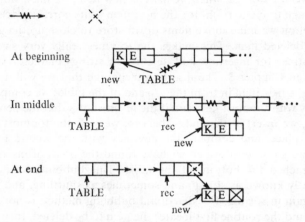

(a) *The three possible positions of insertion. Previous values of pointers which have been changed by the insertion, are shown thus – ⧵⟩ or ⤬.*

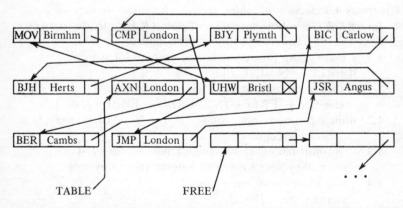

(b) *Sorted table in chained storage, contrasting the logical relationships manifest in the chaining with the physical relationships, contiguity in storage.*

Fig. 4.6. *Insertion into a sorted chained sequential table.*

if the point of insertion is at the beginning of the table. In writing the insertion routines, create a new record, and then insert it in one of three ways, as shown in Fig. 4.6(a). Fig. 4.6(b) shows the result of building up a table of 8 entries using this insertion method: notice how knotted up the chained sequence of the table is, though the logical sequence through the pointers is correct.

ROUTINES 4.4. *Sequential table, sorted, with chained storage*
Exercise.

Both the insertion and deletion routines would be simplified if we used a dummy record at the start of the table, since this would make special test for the start unnecessary. Also, as discussed earlier, a dummy terminating record could be used for enhanced efficiency.

3 Assessment

We now come to assess the effectiveness of these sequential table methods, with their exhaustive search strategies. In the unsorted vector form, Routines 4.1, they are certainly easy to implement. In all forms there is no real difficulty, the most complex procedures being chained storage deletions.

To obtain some idea of the time taken to perform the various operations, let us consider the common part of all the lookup routines, searching for a particular item in the table. At the one extreme we find the item we are after at the beginning of the table, after consideration of only one item (involving accessing the key and comparing it with a given search key), while at the other extreme we must search through every item to find the item we are after at the end of the table, considering all K items on the way. Let us say that on a random occasion the search involves L items before we find the item. L can vary between 1 and K, and let us write the probability that L has the particular value j as $\Pr(L = j)$. What we want to know is the expected value, or average value, of L. We write this $E(L)$, and can calculate it from the formula

$$E(L) = \sum_{j=1}^{K} j \Pr(L = j).$$

103

If we assume that all items are equally likely to be searched for, then $\Pr(L = j) = (1/K)$ and we have $E(L) = (K+1)/2$. We shall later consider situations where this assumption of the uniform distribution on keys is invalid: let us for the moment consider the consequences of the simple formula that we have derived.

We see that for sequential tables (linear tables) the search length is on the average roughly $K/2$. If we double the size of the table, we double the amount of work in using the table. For **small** tables this is alright, and for small tables we would use sequential tables. If no printout is required, then an unsorted table would be appropriate, and the choice must be vector storage Routines 4.1, since chaining provides no advantages. However, if a printout is required, then sorted tables are appropriate, and whether we choose vector or chained storage depends very much upon the relative frequencies of insertions and deletions in comparison with look-ups and updates. With vector storage, insertions and deletions involve a lot of extra work in shifting the items up or down store, while in chaining there is only a small extra involved with the manipulation of pointers. We thus should use vector storage if insertions and deletions do not occur, or only occur relatively infrequently, but use chaining if insertions and deletions are frequent activities. This will be an often repeated conclusion: for changes, use chaining. In summary, we have:

For small tables, use sequential (linear) table.

For no printout, use vector storage, Routines 4.1.

For printout, but few insertions and deletions, use vector storage, Routines 4.3.

For printout, with frequent insertions and deletions, use chained storage, Routines 4.4.

Note that sequential tables are very efficient in their use of storage, in vector storage using the minimum storage necessary for the storage of the complete items, while for chaining there is some extra storage used for pointers.

Our calculations depend completely upon the initial assumption that all keys are equally likely. The figure for insertion does not in fact depend upon this, but the figures for lookup do. What if some keys occur much more often than others? We could argue that on the average this does not make any difference, when we consider all possible choices of key for the table, and all possible placings in the table. But clearly in the unsorted tables, if we place the most frequently used items at the front we would save on search time on the average. This saving can be very significant: to see how significant, let us consider a distribution of keys that is not uniform, letting the probability of the key in position i be $1/(i \cdot c)$ where c is a constant,

$$c = \sum_{j=1}^{K} \frac{1}{j},$$

chosen so that the sum of the probabilities comes to one,

$$\sum_{i=1}^{K} \frac{1}{i \cdot c} = 1.$$

Then the average number of key accesses for lookup is reduced from $(K+1)/2$ to K/c. For K equal to 10, this is a reduction from 5·5 to 3·4, while for K equal to 100, this is a reduction from 50·5 to 19·3. This is considerable saving, and the distribution assumed, a Zipfian distribution, is reasonable. Thus clearly it may often pay to rearrange a table so that the order in the table is in descending order of activity: one way to do this is to keep statistics on usage, and after some time sort the records using the usage counts as the sort key. This is a common strategy, particularly for large sequential files on backing store such as magnetic tape, where the sequential nature of the file has been imposed by the physical nature of the storage medium.

.2 Comparison tree tables

In order to make our tables more efficient, we must arrange to make our paths of access more direct than those seen in the last section. We shall arrange our table as a tree. The general strategy will be to form a tree by dividing the table into subtables, the collection of items into subsets of items. In order to access an item, we first decide which subset to look in, select the correct subset, and then search further.

A set of items, A, is partitioned into subsets $A_1, A_2, \ldots$. The partitioning is made in such a way that all the items of subset A_1 are less than all the items of subset A_2, and so on. For example, for the set of items of Table 4.1, we might partition as follows. Only the keys

105

are shown, but we should imagine that attached to each key is the corresponding entry. The table complete forms the set A,

$$A = \{AXN, BIC, BJH, BJY, CMP, JSR, MOV, UHW\}.$$

These are partitioned initially into three subsets:

$$A_1 = \{AXN, BIC, BJH\} = \{xxx : xxx < BJY\}$$
$$= \{\text{all items } \{xxx \text{ in } A \text{ which are less than BJY}\}.$$
$$A_2 = \{BJY\}$$
$$A_3 = \{CMP, JSR, MOV, UHW\} = \{xxx : xxx > BJY\}.$$

The partitioning continues, as illustrated in Fig. 4.7(d). Note how we have drawn the tree: A_1 has the elements in the left subtree, A_2 has its single element at the root, while A_3 is the set of elements in the right subtree. The same partitioning method extends to the lower levels of the tree. We use the tree by starting at the root, comparing the search key, say BIC, with the key at the root, and then move left or right depending upon whether the search key is less than or greater than the key at the root. If they are equal, we have found the key for which we are searching. Thus we compare BIC with the key at the root, BJY, and move left because BIC is less than BJY. At the next comparison we locate BIC.

In general we have

$$\{\text{left subtree keys}\} < \text{root key} < \{\text{right subtree keys}\}.$$

The strategy for searching such a tree for the occurrence of a key K is:

ALGORITHM 4.5. *Searching a comparison tree*
1. Search(T,K); ¢ searches comparison tree T for item with key K ¢
   1.1. **if** tree T empty **then** [error—item not in table, **Exit**]
   1.2.   **else if** key K at root of T **then** [success, **Exit**]
   1.3.   **else if** key K is less than root of T
              then [move down to left, search left subtree for K]
              else [move down to right, search right subtree for K]

This has been expressed recursively, but is best implemented by looping: a stack is not necessary since once we have decided on which subtree to search, then we know we will never regret that decision and need to back-track.

Because of the role of comparisons in the use of this tree, we shall call such trees **comparison trees**. There are two variations of comparison trees, one for vector storage, and one for chained storage. Superficially these two methods look so different that they are not commonly associated. We shall study each method in turn, and then consider variations on the chained method which make the association clear.

1 Comparison trees in vector storage with log search

Let us initially consider storing the tree in vector storage. We have already seen the method, in section 2.1.2, where the edges of the tree were implicit in relationships between addresses, and movements along the edges involved address arithmetic.

Suppose that the keys are stored in vector KEY$[i:j]$. Then we make the root of the tree at KEY$[m]$, where $m = \lfloor(i+j)/2\rfloor$ (i.e., the largest integer less than or equal to $(i+j)/2$). The left subtree is stored in KEY$[i:m-1]$, and the right subtree is stored in KEY$[m+1:j]$. This is shown in Fig. 4.7.

Now if we apply this storage technique to Algorithm 4.5, we obtain the search Routines 4.6 given below: this is much more familiar as an 'extra' method for searching sorted sequential tables in vector storage, but properly belongs to the tree table methods.

ROUTINES 4.6. *Log search or binary search*
1. Log search(KEY,i,j,K); ¢ searches vector KEY$[i:j]$ for key K ¢
   ¢ uses a tree structured search, as Algorithm 4.5 ¢
   1.1. **while** $i \leq j$ **do**
   1.2. ₁$[m \leftarrow \lfloor(i+j)/2\rfloor$; ¢ index of root of tree ¢
   1.3. **if** KEY$[m] = K$ **then** [¢ success ¢ **Result** ← m; **Exit.**]
   1.4. **else if** KEY$[m] < K$
   1.5. **then** [¢ search left ¢ $j \leftarrow m-1$;]
   1.6. **else** [¢ search right ¢ $i \leftarrow m+1$;]
   ]₁
   1.7. ¢ error—not in table ¢ **Exit.**

Consider the example of Fig. 4.7(c), and consider looking up the entry of key BJH. Initially we are searching for BJH in KEY$[1:8]$.

(a)

Offset	Key
1	AXN
2	BIC
3	BJY
4	CMP
5	JSR
6	MOV
7	UHW

(b)

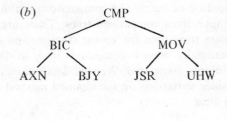

(c)

Offset	Key
1	AXN
2	BIC
3	BJH
4	BJY
5	CMP
6	JSR
7	MOV
8	UHR

(d)

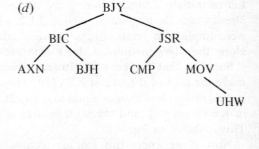

Fig. 4.7. Comparison tree, with vector storage and log search. The tree stored in vect [i : j] *has root at* $k = \lfloor (i+j)/2 \rfloor$.

(a) *Seven keys in vector storage, sorted.*
(b) *Corresponding tree.*
(c) *An 8th key added, vector storage.* (d) *Corresponding tree.*

The root is at KEY[4]. Compare BJH with KEY[4] = BJY. BJH is less, so we search for BJH in KEY[1 : 3]. The root at the half-way point is at KEY[2]. Compare BJH with KEY[2] = BIC. BJH is larger, so we must search for BJH in KEY[3 : 3]. The root of this degenerate tree is at KEY[3]. We compare them and find a match. We have found the position of BJH in the table, and can now extract its entry.

Referring to the tree of Fig. 4.7(d), we see that we move down the tree, first to the left, then to the right, and so to the match of keys at the leaf.

Now consider Fig. 4.7(a), and add BJH to this to form Fig. 4.7(c).

The procedure involves finding the point of insertion, and then shifting the data down the vector to make room for the new record, as we did in vector sorted sequential tables, Routines 4.3. This completely changes the tree! Compare Figs. 4.7(b) and 4.7(d). Of course the change in the tree does not change the basic log search routine. The significance of the observation, that insertion (and for that matter, deletion) completely transforms and restructures the comparison tree, will become apparent later when we consider the chaining method for comparison trees.

ROUTINES 4.7. *Comparison tree table in vector storage*
These are all base on logsearch or binary search, Routines 4.6, and are left as an exercise.

How good is logsearch? At each step in the search we roughly cut in half the size of the table in which we are searching, and must therefore reach a table of size 1 in roughly $\log_2 K$ steps, where K is the size of the table. Hence the name logsearch. More accurately, the number of key accesses or comparisons for a successful look-up operation is $(1+(1/K))\log_2(K+1)-1$, but the important property is that the result is of order $\log_2 K$. If we double the size of the table we only add 1 one key accessing and comparison operation! However, for insertions and deletions we are still saddled with the requirement to shift the items up or down storage, and that involves an amount of work of order K, and we are really no better off than we were with sequential tables. We thus conclude that logsearch comparison tables are only good where lookup and update are the dominant activities: that is, the table has a fixed content. In forming up the tables we might as well use the simple bubble insertion of Routines 4.3. Thus in summary we have:
For medium to large fixed tables, use logsearch.

.2 Comparison trees with chaining

Can we, by using chaining, obtain an efficient insertion and deletion operation, of order $\log_2 K$? Let us go straight in and see how we can store the comparison tree using chaining. Fig. 4.8(a) shows the basic record, with four fields, two for the Key and Entry, and two more

LEFT	KEY	ENTRY	RIGHT

(a) *The record and its component fields.*

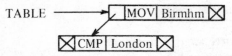

(b) *The TABLE started empty, and has now had MOV inserted.*

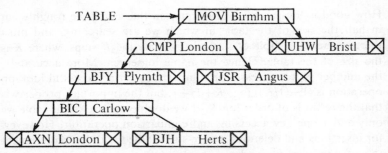

(c) *The item with CMP as key has been added.*

(d) *The complete tree table after 8 items have been added.*

Fig. 4.8. *Using chaining for comparison tree tables.*

for pointers to the left and right subtrees. Fig. 4.8(*b*) shows a tree containing a single node. Let us add a second node to the tree: let us add CMP to the tree. We compare it with MOV, it is less, so we must insert CMP to the left. The left pointer is empty, so we place CMP and its associated entry in a new record with a pointer in the left field of the MOV record, pointing to the CMP record. This is shown in Fig. 4.8(*c*). To insert BJY we would compare with the root key, MOV, follow down the left pointer, compare BJY with CMP, go left, find it empty and then insert a record containing BJY, and so on.

The general insertion algorithm is given below. It leads eventually to the diagram of Fig. 4.8(*d*).

110

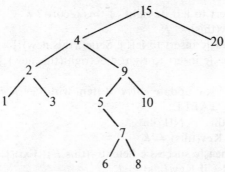

(a) Before deletion of the 4.

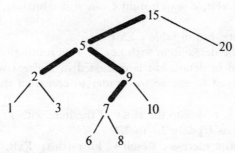

(b) After deletion of the 4, replacing it by the 5.

Fig. 4.9. Example illustrating a deletion from a comparison tree table, with chained storage of the tree.

ROUTINES 4.8. *Comparison tree tables with chaining*

1. Insert(K,E); ¢ insert item (K,E) into tree TABLE ¢
   1.1. ¢ create new record to be inserted later ¢
        new ← Cons(NIL,K,E,NIL);
   1.2. **if** ¢ table empty ¢ TABLE = NIL
   1.3.   **then**$_1$[¢ insert as new table ¢ TABLE ← new; **Exit**]$_1$
   1.4. next ← TABLE;
   1.5. **while** next ≠ NIL **do**
   1.6. $_2$[this ← next;
   1.7.   **if** Key(this) < K
   1.8.   **then**$_3$[¢ search left ¢ next←Left(this);]$_3$
   1.9.   **else**$_4$[¢ search right ¢ next←Right(this);]$_4$
            ]$_2$

111

1.10. ¢ insert to left or right of this record? ¢
       if key(this) < K
1.11.   **then₅**[¢ insert to left ¢ Setleft(this,new);]₅
1.12.   **else₆**[¢ insert to right ¢ Setright(this,new);]₆
1.12. **Exit.**
2. Update(K,E); ¢ update entry of item with key K ¢
   2.1. this ← TABLE;
   2.2. **while** this ≠ NIL **do**
   2.3.   ₁[**if** Key(this) = K
   2.4.   **then₂**[¢ success ¢ Setentry(this,E); **Exit.**]₂
   2.5.   **else if** Key(this) < K
   2.5.   **then₃**[¢ search left ¢ this ← Left(this);]₃
   2.6.   **else₄**[¢ search right ¢ this ← Right(this);]₄
           ]₁
   2.7. ¢ error—not in table ¢ **Exit.**
3. Delete(K); ¢ delete item with key K. This routine is too complex
   to be given in detail, but is discussed in the text where enough
   detail is given to enable the reader to construct the routine for
   himself ¢
4. Lookup(K); ¢ lookup the entry of the item with key K ¢
   4.1 to 4.3. as Update 2.1 to 2.3
   4.4.   **then₂**[¢ success ¢ **Result** ← Entry(this); **Exit.**]₂
   4.5 to 4.7. as Update 2.5 to 2.7.
5. Printout(T); ¢ prints out the complete table in order ¢
   ¢ uses an in-order tree traversal ¢
   5.1. **if** T = NIL **then Exit**
   5.2.   **else₁**[Printout(Left(T));
   5.3.   Printkey(T); Printentry(T);
   5.4.   Printout(Right(T));]₁
¢ Auxiliary storage management and record accessing routines ¢
6. Initialise; ¢ chain free list using Left fields ¢
   ¢ see Routines 2.2 ¢
7. Cons(A,B,C,Dɟ); ¢ constructs a new record, obtaining the next
   record off the free list; filling in the field values ¢
   ¢ see Routines 2.6 ¢
8. Return(R); ¢ returns record R to free list ¢
   ¢ see Routines 2.3 ¢
9. Key(R), Entry(R), Left(R), Right(R), Setentry(R,E), Setleft(R,P)
   and Setright(R,P) field accessing and updating routines.

112

10. Printkey(R) and Printentry(R) routines for printing key and entry of record R.

We have already seen how the insertion routine works, and how as it is repeatedly applied it builds a tree as shown in Fig. 4.8. Lookup and update both use the tree structured search of Algorithm 4.5 and are obvious. Printout involves a tree traversal, an in-order tree traversal. This tree traversal has been expressed recursively, but could have done using a stack as in Algorithm 1.4, Fig. 1.10, or by using extra pointers as in Algorithm 1.5, Fig. 1.11. Notice how the emptiness of the tree at step 5.1 is simply determined by T being the null pointer NIL.

It is the deletion routine which provides the real complexities. If deletions are not required, as often will be the case (e.g. assembler and compiler symbol tables) then the deletion routine is superfluous and the storage management routines also become simpler, there being no need for a free list, the methods of Routines 2.1 sufficing. However, if we do require to delete items from the table, it is possible with not much more effort than that required for the insertion routine! Firstly we must locate the record to be removed, recording at the same time the 'parent' record (thus deletion of the root will require special treatment). Having located this record for removal, we now find a record further down the tree to replace it: we find either the next largest item in the table, the leftmost record to the right, or alternatively the next smallest item, the rightmost to the left. Cases needing special treatment occur when either the left subtree or the right subtree below the deleted record are empty. The actual replacement operation requires the adjustment of pointers in the parent record, in the replacing record, and in the parent of the replacing record. The reader may think up alternative methods that seem to involve less work, but be warned: you could spoil the tree and make it less effective and efficient for later operations! We shall come back to this consideration later. Fig. 4.9 shows an example of deletion. The edges of the tree changed by the deletion are drawn in heavy lines.

We must now consider how efficient the comparison trees with chaining are. In terms of storage, for every item we have an extra two pointers: depending upon the relative sizes of the key, entry, and pointers, this could be an insignificant extra, or of great

113

significance. To assess speed we shall need to consider how many keys must we on the average access before we find the position in the tree that we want, and have executed all the operations necessary. Our main concern is the order of the work involved: is it of order K, of order $\log_2 K$, or what?

The trees that we obtain by repeated applications of the insert operation can vary a great deal: we have seen some examples in Figs. 4.8 and 4.9. If the data has been presented in the order AXN, UHW, MOV, JSR, BIC, CMP, BJY, then a highly degenerate tree would have resulted. It would be linear, and no better than sequential tables; searching this tree on the average is worse than for sequential tables, since in the search we have tests to see if we move left or right. However, had the data been presented in the order CMP, MOV, BIC, JSR, UHW, BJY, AXN, then the tree of Fig. 4.7(*a*) would have resulted: this is the kind of tree we obtained in logsearch and as we have argued, involves of order $\log_2 K$ key accesses. Clearly the tree that we obtain depends critically on the order in which the items are presented to the insertion routine, and we must consider what happens on the average, when we consider all possible orders of presentation. It turns out that the average is of order $\log_2 K$! This very interesting result was obtained by Hibbard in 1962 and is proved in the following theorem.

THEOREM 4.1. (*Hibbard*)
For a comparison tree table containing K items chained, the average search length (number of items encountered) for insertion is

$$P(K) = 2 \left(\frac{1}{2} + \frac{1}{3} + \frac{1}{4} + \ldots + \frac{1}{K+1} \right)$$

and the average search length for look-up, update, and deletion is

$$Q(K) = \frac{K+1}{K} \cdot P(K) - 1.$$

The average is taken over all possible orders of presentation of the items in the formation of the tree.

Proof. Let us redraw our trees so as to emphasise the points of insertion. This has been done in Fig. 4.10: the points of insertion

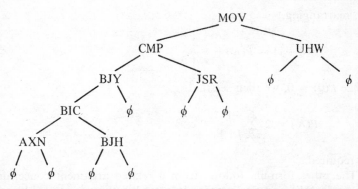

Fig. 4.10. The tree of Fig. 4.8(d) showing the points of insertion (these are the null pointers), shown as the leaves ɸ. There are 8 internal nodes, and 9 leaves.

are the leaves of the pure binary tree, marked ϕ. For K items in the tree, there are K *internal nodes* (non-leaf nodes) and $K+1$ leaves. For K items this is always true and is easily proved by induction.

Finding a point of insertion means starting from the root of the tree, and progressing from there to a leaf ϕ. The search length for a particular insertion is the length of the path from root to the leaf where the insertion will be made (i.e. number of edges traversed or number of internal nodes passed). For a tree of K internal nodes, there are $K+1$ possible insertion search paths from root to leaf. We shall assume that in considering the insertion of a $(K+1)$th item, all possible insertion points are equally likely. For an average point of insertion in an average tree, the path length is just $P(K)$ by definition, and the total insertion path length in an average tree is then

$$p(K) = (K+1)P(K).$$

Adding a $(K+1)$th item to the tree means replacing a leaf by a node with edges to two leaves: thus one path length L is removed and replaced by two of length $L+1$, and the total path length has been increased by $L+2$. On the average L is $P(K)$, and thus we obtain the recursive relationship for $P(K)$

$$
\begin{aligned}
p(K+1) &= (K+2)P(K+1) \\
&= p(K)+P(K)+2 = (K+1)P(K)+P(K)+2 \\
&= (K+2)P(K)+2,
\end{aligned}
$$

115

or, rearranging,

$$P(K+1) = P(K) + \frac{2}{K+2}.$$

Since $P(0) = 0$, we then see that

$$P(K) = 2 \sum_{i=1}^{K} \frac{1}{i+1}$$

as required.

The other formula follows from a related argument concerning internal paths and the increase in total length when an additional item is added to the table.

COROLLARY. $P(K)$ is bounded as follows:

$$2 \log_e \left(\frac{K}{2} + 1 \right) < P(K) < 2 \log_e(K+1) = 1.4 \log_2(K+1)$$

Proof. This follows from noting that $P(K)$ is approximated by $\int \frac{dx}{x}$ over a suitable range. In fact, we have

$$\int_{2}^{K+2} \frac{dx}{x} < \frac{1}{2} P(K) < \int_{1}^{K+1} \frac{dx}{x}$$

from which the result follows.

(Adapted from Hibbard, T. N., 'Some combinatorial properties of certain trees, with applications to searching and sorting', *Journal A.C.M.*, vol. 9, no. 1 (January 1962), pp. 13–28.)

Thus we see that on the average insertions build up a tree which has a search length of order $\log_2 K$. This is the same as logsearch, though a detailed inspection of the formula shows a factor of 1·4 against chained comparison trees. Now we come back to the earlier comment about deletions: insertions on the average build more-or-less balanced trees, and the deletion method used must not upset this. The method given was shown by Hibbard to, on the average, not upset the balancing. Programming complexity is somewhat greater than for logsearch, especially if the deletion capability is included.

In summary, we conclude that for medium to large tables which dynamically change through insertions and deletions, use comparison trees with chaining.

3 Balancing chained comparison trees

We shall now compare the chained and the vector comparison trees. With chaining as presented in the last section we see that, though on the average the efficiencies are of order $\log_2 K$, the worst case is of order $K/2$. We resorted to chaining in the hope that we could do as well as logsearch for lookup and improve on insertions and deletions—we succeeded, but only by having something of a gamble. But log search has no variation in efficiency—how does it do this? Consider again Fig. 4.7: on insertion, the tree was effectively completely restructured to maintain balancing. A tree would be balanced if the longest path from root to leaf (insertion leaf ϕ as in Fig. 4.10), and the shortest path from root to leaf, differed at most by only 1. Such is the case in Fig. 4.7, and the shifting operation ensures that this balancing is maintained on both insertions and deletions. But note that in some measure the vector restructuring overdoes it, for not only does it rebalance, it also makes the longer path always lie to the right.

With chained comparison trees we can also restructure the trees to maintain balancing. By not overdoing it as in logsearch, we shall be able to achieve the rebalancing at a cost of order $\log_2 K$ and not $K/2$ as in logsearch! To achieve the balancing we must maintain markers at each node to indicate whether the tree is balanced or unbalanced with too much to the right or the left. Now on insertion and deletion we must not only compare keys, but must also inspect the balancing markers. The actual algorithms are quite complex and we shall not consider them further, though the interested reader could try to invent them for himself, consulting the paper by Martin and Ness for one solution (Martin, W. A., and Ness, D. N., 'Optimising binary trees grown with a sorting algorithm', *Communications A.C.M.*, vol. 15, no. 2 (February 1972), pp. 88–93.)

117

4.1.3 Address calculation tables

The idea here is to use the key as an address, or derive in some way an address from the key, and store the item in the record indicated by the address. The simplest idea is to have a unique address for each possible key: that is the idea in direct access tables, but this can be inefficient, and the overcoming of the storage inefficiencies leads to the hashing technique. With address calculation tables we attain an access structure identical to, or very close to, the basic tree structure of the table considered originally in Fig. 4.2.

4.1.3.1 Direct access tables

Suppose that we have **n** possible keys. Then given a key k we calculate an address from k in the range 0 to $n-1$. Let us look at our example.

In our example of Table 4.1, there are altogether 26^3 possible keys composed of three letters, and thus for the direct access table we must set aside $26^3 = 17,576$ storage slots for the entries. We do

Key	Codes of letters $A = 0, \ldots, Z = 25$			Address
MOV	12	14	21	8497
CMP	2	12	15	1679
BJY	1	9	24	934
BIC	1	8	2	886
BJH	1	9	7	917
AXN	0	23	13	611
UHW	20	7	22	13724
JSR	9	18	17	6569

Table 4.2. Example illustrating direct access tables: for each three letter key the corresponding address is calculated, using formula address = (code of first letter) × 26^2 + (code of second letter) × 26 + (code of third letter).

Key	Codes of letters $A = 0, \ldots, Z = 25$			Hash address
MOV	12	14	21	7
CMP	2	12	15	9
BJY	1	9	24	8
BIC	1	8	2	1
BJH	1	9	7	7
AXN	0	23	13	6
UHW	20	7	22	9
JSR	9	18	17	4

Table 4.3. Example, illustrating hash addressing. Addresses are computed from the three-letter key by adding together the codes of the letters and taking the remainder on division by 10.

not need to store the keys, since these are uniquely related to the addresses, and can be reconstructed from them. Then, for example, we store the entry of MOV at the $12*26^2 + 14*26 + 21 = 8497$th slot. Table 4.2 shows the keys for our example, the codes for the characters, and the resulting offset in the table. Inserting an item means calculating the offset, and then moving the entry to the position indicated, with the other operations proceeding in similar manner. Printout is possible if the ordering of the addresses is the same as the ordering of the keys, as is the case in our example.

The whole method is very fast: we go directly to the correct place in store to locate the entry. But it can be disastrously inefficient in its use of storage. Our example is such a case. Sometimes direct access tables are good, for example for tabular functions in numerical analysis.

.2 Hash tables

The natural development of direct access tables, is to compute an address not in the full range 0 to $n-1$, but in some more restricted range. The method is then known as hash addressing, hash coding, or scatter storage, and sometimes even as content-addressing. We shall stick to hash addressing as the most meaningful name for the method.

In the simple direct access table, we had **n** possible keys, and for each of these could generate a unique address in the range 0 to **n**−1. However, if only K keys actually occur, and $K \ll \mathbf{n}$, then we waste a lot of storage. So now let us calculate an address in some smaller range, say 0 to $N-1$, where $K < N \ll \mathbf{n}$. This means that different keys may lead to the same address, and thus we run the risk of putting two different items into the same storage slot, but there are ways of handling this.

Let us look at our example. For the eight items we shall set aside only 10 slots, so $K = 8$ and $N = 10$. We shall calculate a hash address from the key in the range 0 to 9 by adding together the decimal numeric codes for the three characters comprising the key, and then taking the remainder after division by 10 (that is, the residue modulo 10). The resulting hash addresses are shown in Table 4.3. Now, as the data is input, we compute from the key the hash address, and then store the item (key,entry) at the corresponding slot in the table. Thus (MOV,Birmhm) goes into the 7th position (storage record), (CMP,London) goes into record 9, and so on until BJH is encountered. The situation at this point is shown in Fig. 4.11(*a*). The hash of BJH is 7, and thus BJH should go in record 7; but record 7 is already occupied, BJH *collides* with MOV, and we must in some way resolve this collision by finding somewhere else to store (BJH,Herts). What we shall do is to scan forwards from a collision until we find a free record in which to place the new item: as we scan forwards we may reach the end of the table, in which case we 'wrap around' and start scanning from the start of the table. The hash address of BIS was 7, and record 7 was occupied, so we try record 8. This is also occupied, as is record 9, at which point we have reached the end of the table and wrap around to try record 0. Record 0 is empty, so we insert the new item (BJH,Herts) there. The next key is AXN which hashes to record 6 which is empty, and so no complications. The next key, UHW, hashes to record 9 which is occupied, so we have a collision which is resolved by scanning forwards, wrapping around and eventually leading to the insertion of (UHW,Bristol) in record 2. Finally JSR hashes

Record number	Key	Entry
0		
1	BIC	Carlow
2		
3		
4		
5		
6		
7	MOV	Birmhm
8	BJY	Plymth
9	CMP	London

(a) The table after inserting 4 items, just before the first collision occurs.

Record number	Key	Entry
0	BJH	Herts
1	BIC	Carlow
2	UHW	Bristl
3		
4	JSR	Angus
5		
6	AXN	London
7	MOV	Birmhm
8	BJY	Plymth
9	CMP	London

(b) The table after insertion of all 8 items.

Fig. 4.11. Example of hash tables, using a linear rehash to resolve collisions. The initial hashes are as in Table 4.3, while the rehash function is $h \leftarrow h + 1$ (10).

121

to record 4 without collision. The final situation is shown in Fig. 4.11(*b*).

How do we lookup an item? We simply repeat the process we went through for insertion, calculating an initial hash, and then testing keys for a match, scanning forwards until either a match is found, or we run into an empty record. In our example, Fig. 4.11(*b*), let us lookup BJH. This hashes to record 7, where we inspect the key: the key is not BJH but neither is it empty (it is MOV), so we take the action we took previously on resolving collisions, and scan forwards to the next record, number 8, where the keys don't match, and so on until a match is located at record 0.

The way in which we calculated our hash addresses is not the only way, and we shall discuss alternatives later. Also the way we resolved collisions is by no means the only way: the basic requirement of the **rehashing** operation is that it should compute a new hash address in the range 0 to $N-1$, and as it is repeated it should compute all possible addresses in the range 0 to $N-1$ before returning to where it started from. This will be discussed in more detail after the presentation of the table routines.

Instead of rehashing to resolve collisions, we could maintain an **overflow** area of storage, using chaining to keep together all the items that hash to a particular position. Thus we would use storage records with three fields, one for the Key, one for the Entry, and one for a pointer to the next record in the sequence. The two main alternatives are shown in Fig. 4.12: we either have a primary table of pointers only which lead us into the overflow area where all the records are managed; or we set aside the first part of the record storage as the primary table area and chain from there further into the record area where overflows are maintained. As always, chaining means extra storage, but has some advantages concerning insertions and deletions, as well as being somewhat faster than the rehash methods, since the colliding items are kept separate. Note that we do not require that $K \leq N$ for the chaining method.

There is the further possibility that the two methods, rehashing and chaining, could be mixed, but we shall ignore that possibility, as well as many other variations on the hashing idea.

Let us now consider in more detail and generality the two basic hash table methods, starting with the rehashing method for the resolution of collisions, then a discussion of the hash and rehash

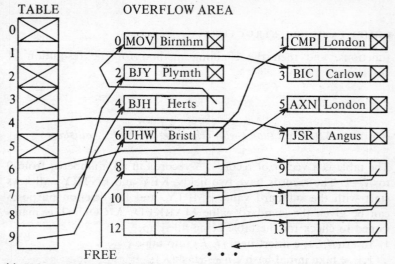

(a) Using a primary table of pointers which lead into an overflow area.

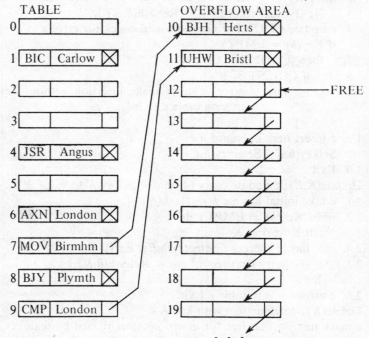

(b) Using a primary table of records, which lead to an overflow area which is an extension of the table.

Fig. 4.12. Example of hash tables, resolving collisions by chaining into an overflow area. Example of Table 4.3.

123

functions, and then the chaining method for the resolution of collisions.

ROUTINES 4.9. *Hash tables with rehashing to resolve collisions*

The table is a vector of records, N records in all, numbered from 0 to $N-1$. The records have two fields, KEY and ENTRY. All keys start with the standard value EMPTY, and for deletion purposes can be given the standard value MARKED. A COUNT is maintained to check for the table being filled up.

1. Insert(K,E); ¢ insert item (K,E) into table ¢
   1.1. ¢ take initial hash ¢ $h \leftarrow$ Hash(K);
   1.2. **while** Key$(h) \neq$ EMPTY **or** Key$(h) \neq$ MARKED **do**
   1.3. $_1$[¢ try next record ¢ $h \leftarrow$ Rehash(h,K);]$_1$
   1.4. ¢ update COUNT if necessary and check for error ¢
       if Key$(h) =$ EMPTY
   1.5.   **then**$_2$[COUNT $\leftarrow$ COUNT$+1$;
   1.6.   **if** COUNT $= N$
   1.7.   **then**$_3$[¢ error—cannot make insertion without destroying table ¢ **Exit**.]$_3$
        ]$_2$
   1.8. ¢ insert item in record h ¢
       Setkey(h,K); Setentry(h,E);
   1.9. **Exit**.
2. Update(K,E); ¢ update entry of item with key K to value E ¢
   2.1. ¢ take initial has h ¢ $h \leftarrow$ Hash(K);
   2.2. **while** Key$(h) \neq$ EMPTY **do**
   2.3. $_1$[**if** Key$(h) = K$
   2.4.   **then**[¢ success ¢ Setentry(h,E); **Exit**]
   2.5.   **else**[¢ try next record ¢ $h \leftarrow$ Rehash(h,K):]
       ]$_1$
   2.6. ¢ error—not in table ¢ **Exit**.
3. Delete(K); ¢ delete item with key K ¢
   ¢ mark item so that free for insertions, but passed by searches ¢
   3.1 to 3.3. as Update 2.1 to 2.3
   3.4.   **then**[¢ success ¢ Setkey$(h,$MARKED$)$; **Exit**]
   3.5 to 3.6. as Update 2.5 to 2.6.

4. Lookup(K); ¢ lookup the entry of item with key K ¢
    4.1 to 4.3. as Update 2.1 to 2.3
    4.4.   **then**[¢ success ¢ **Result** ← Entry(h); **Exit**]
    4.5 to 4.6. as Update 2.5 to 2.6.

5. Printout; ¢ prints out all the items in the table in ascending order
of key. Only possible if the Hash function is order preserving,
and on insertion ordering is taken into account, with a simple
linear rehash of $h \leftarrow h \pm 1$ without wrap around. Other routines
are also complicated ¢

¢ Auxiliary routines ¢

6. Hash(K); ¢ from key K computes an integer in range 0 to $N-1$,
uniformly distributed. Specific examples will be found in the
text. ¢

7. Rehash(h,K); ¢ calculates a new hash address from the previous
hash, and possibly the key K. Must generate a full cycle of the
integers 0 through $N-1$ before repeating any integer. Specific
examples will be found in the text. ¢

8. Initialise; ¢ clear the table, setting all keys to EMPTY and
COUNT = 0 ¢

9. Key, Entry, Setkey, Setentry, field accessing and updating functions for the records, details depending upon particular methods
of storage.

Observe how close Routines 4.9.2, 4.9.3, and 4.9.4 are, and they
could well be replaced by a single search routine which returns the
address of the record sought.

We must now fill in details concerning the critically important
functions Hash(K) and Rehash(h,K). These ought to be arranged
to make the table as efficient as possible. Ideally the Hash function
should calculate a unique address for each of the keys that actually
appear, thus making the Rehash function redundant! For fixed
tables with some effort a suitable function can usually be found. But
for tables that are not fixed, where the possible keys are taken from
some large population, no perfect hash function exists, and we
require one which is on the average good, when we take into account
the way that keys occur in practice, the distribution of keys, and the
dependencies between them. We require that the hash addresses are
spread out uniformly throughout the table, and departures from

this is known as 'primary clustering', when many keys hash to the same (or adjacent) positions in the table. Combined with the choice of Hash function is the choice of the precise size of the table. There are three principle methods for hash functions, assuming that the key occupies a single machine word of storage (if it occupies more than one word combine the component words into a single word by adding them together, or exclusive-OR-ing them together). The first method is to use a table of a size which is a power of 2 (64, 128, 256, etc.) and compute the hash address by a 'mid-square' technique of squaring the key (thought of as a number) and then selecting the central bits as the Hash. The second method is to divide the key by N and take the remainder: N is chosen to ensure that all bits of the key play a role in the formation of the hash, and thus taking N as a power of 2 is disastrous, and usually a prime number would be selected (this also has advantages for Rehashing, as will be seen). The third method is related to the first in that the key is multiplied by a constant (relatively prime to machine word size) and some central bits selected (for example, the most significant bits of the least significant word of the product).

Let us now turn to our example, in Fig. 4.11. The hash function here combines the components of the key into a single number, adding the codes together, and then uses the second hashing method, taking the remainder on division by 10 (this value was chosen for simplicity of exposition, and is not good). This hashing function shows a primary cluster around records 7 to 9. The rehashing method of incrementing the initial hash then suffers because of this cluster, since a collision at the bottom of the cluster must step right through the cluster before finding an empty record. This happened on the first collision. But our rehash also suffers because of a more subtle effect: the second collision also in the primary cluster (hash $= 9$) steps across BIS which was placed in record 0 at the first collision. The rehashing operations starting as record 7 and those starting at record 9 become combined, and the number of rehashes required is bigger because of this. This phenomenon is known as a secondary clustering, and can be tackled independently of primary clustering.

Thus the requirements of the rehash function are that it generates on repeated application a complete sequence of rehash addresses between 0 and $N-1$, and also that it solves the secondary clustering problem. The simplest form of rehashing, linear rehashing, where hash h has a constant added or subtracted,

$$h \leftarrow h + p \quad (N)$$

meets the first requirement if p and N are relatively prime (that is, they have no common factor other than 1), which is clearly the case for any p if N is prime. If $p = 1$, we run foul of any primary clustering, which can be overcome by using a value of p substantially greater than 1: we can never overcome the effect of secondary clustering because once the sequence of rehashes combine, they stay combined. There are three methods of overcoming secondary clustering in common use: these are **double hash**, and **quadratic rehash**, and **random rehash**. In double rehash, we use a method very similar to linear rehash, but use as the increment p a value which is obtained by a second hashing operation on the key: if N is prime, then a suitable method is to take the remainder after dividing the key K by any integer less than N (the primeness of N ensures that the cycle of rehashes is complete). A simpler form of this double rehash is to use the original hash h itself plus 1 as the second hash, or perhaps to use $N-h$. (Note that for efficiency this rehashing method requires minor modifications to our general routines.) In quadratic rehash the original initial hash has values ai^2+bi+c successively added, where i is the number of rehash operations previously performed on this search. The drawback with quadratic rehash is that unless table size N and the constants a, b, and c are carefully chosen, a complete cycle of rehashes will not be achieved. In random rehash, a sequence of rehash increments to the initial hash are made using a pseudo-random number generator: the generator must be full cycle. Because double hash is such a satisfactory method, and both quadratic and random rehash are tricky because of the full cycle requirement, double hashing is the preferred method. (*Note*. All the rehashing methods require that the new hash address is reduced to the range 0 to $N-1$. Invariably this does **not** require division, but simply a test to see whether the new hash greater than or equal to N, in which case N is subtracted, or when the increments are negative, a test for N less than 0, in which case N is added to the new hash.)

If we wish to printout the table, without a separate sorting operation, then the table items must appear in ascending order within storage. To ensure this requires both that the initial hashing function

127

is order preserving, and that we use a linear rehash with increment of one, making our insertions so as to preserve ordering. These requirements may well be incompatible with the other requirements of the hash and rehash functions, leading to inefficiency (but, as we shall see, this is not sufficiently deterring to prevent hash tables being the basis of a very attractive sorting method, known as address calculation sorting). In addition, the need to preserve ordering considerably complicates insertion, especially when an insertion attempts to move data above or below the table limits, since we cannot wrap around. To obtain some idea of the complexities let us consider the general search process: on making the initial hash, we compare keys and if the search is less, we then start to scan downwards, while if the search key is greater, we then start to scan upwards. The search continues until either an empty key is encountered, or a comparison shows that we have gone too far. We can avoid testing for the table limits by putting dummy records below and above with keys respectively being the smallest possible and the largest possible.

An important special case of order preserving hashing is 'decoding'. A key consisting of several symbols has the first symbol used as the hash address, with chaining resolution of collisions (see below).

When on an insertion the capacity of the table is found to have been exceeded, we have taken an error exit. We could alternatively reform the table with a larger allocation of storage, possibly at the same time changing the hash and rehash functions if these were found to be inadequate.

We now consider the alternative method for the resolution of collisions, chaining. This removes all the problems about the selection of rehash functions, but we still require that the initial hash function distributes the hashes uniformly throughout the table. We shall only give the routines for one of the two chained methods of Fig. 4.12, that of Fig. 4.12(a) using a primary table of pointers only. This method of storage has advantages in both insertion and deletion, especially where ordering of the chains is required, but does have the disadvantage of requiring an additional use of a pointer on searches, and an extra amount of storage for the N pointers of the primary table.

Routines 4.10. *Hash tables with chaining to resolve collisions*
The table consists of a primary table of N pointers TABLE[$0 : N-1$]

which is accessed on the initial hash, plus an overflow area where records of three fields, KEY, ENTRY, and NEXT, where the items are stored in chained sequences, each chain being effectively a miniature sequential table.

1. Insert(K,E); ¢ insert item (K,E) into table ¢
   1.1. ¢ initial hash ¢ h ← Hash(K);
   1.2. TABLE[h] ← Cons(K,E,TABLE[h]);
   1.3. **Exit.**

2. Update(K,E); ¢ update entry of item with key K to value E ¢
   2.1. ¢ initial hash ¢ h ← Hash(K);
   2.2. h ← TABLE[h];
   2.3. **while** h ≠ NIL **do**
   2.4. $_1$[**if** Key(h) = K
   2.5.   **then**$_2$[¢ success ¢ Setentry(h,E); **Exit.**]$_2$
   2.6.   **else**$_3$[¢ try next record ¢ h ← Next(h);]$_3$
                ]$_1$
   2.7. ¢ error—not in table ¢ **Exit.**

3. Delete(K); ¢ delete item with key K ¢
   3.1. ¢ initial hash ¢ h ← Hash(K);
   3.2 to 3.12. as sequential chained tables, unsorted, routines 4.2, steps 3.1 to 3.11, with change that instead of TABLE, use TABLE[h].

4. Lookup(K); ¢ lookup entry of item with key K ¢
   4.1 to 4.4. as Update 2.1 to 2.4
   4.5.   **then**$_2$[success ¢ Result ← Entry(h); **Exit**]$_2$
   4.6 to 4.7. as Update 2.6 to 2.7.

5. Printout; ¢ prints out all the items in the table, in ascending order of key. This requires that the initial hash is order preserving, and that on insertion order is preserved within the chains. For details of how to make the changes, see sequential chained sorted tables, Routines 4.4 ¢

¢ Auxiliary routines ¢

6. Hash(K); ¢ as Routines 4.9 ¢

7. Initialise; ¢ sets all the pointers in the primary table to NIL, forms up the free list ¢

8. Cons(A,B,C); ¢ record constructor, obtaining next record from free list, and inserting in the fields the values A, B, and C respectively ¢

129

9. Key, Entry, Next, Setkey, Setentry, Setnext, field accessing and
   updating routines.

Observe how the hash table with chaining to resolve collisions
effectively divides the K items of the table into N miniature chained
sequential tables. (*Note.* We could indeed use any of our table
techniques on these miniature tables, even another round of hashing
—but will not pursue these possibilities, though they should be
remembered.) Having selected the correct sequential subtable, the
work involved follows that of the simple sequential tables: on the
average there are K/N items in each subtable, and thus on the
average we must consult approximately $K/2N$ items to find the one
that we want. The significance of this result is that the time taken is
a function on the ratio $\alpha = K/N$, the **packing density** in the table.
If we double the number of items in the table but keep the packing
density the same, the time taken to retrieve an average item remains
the same!

A closer analysis of hash tables with chaining to resolve collisions,
shows that the average number of key accesses (often called **probes**)
required is

$$1 + \frac{K-1}{2N} \approx 1 + \frac{\alpha}{2}.$$

We prove this important result in the following theorem.

THEOREM 4.2. In hash tables with chaining to resolve collisions, the
average number of keys accesses or probes required to lookup an
item is $1 + (K-1)/2N$, assuming that initial hashes are uniformly
distributed between 0 and $N-1$, and that on lookup all items in the
table are equally likely to be searched for.

Proof. Suppose that the search key hashes to position h, where k
items are placed.

Certainly $k \geq 1$ (because the search key certainly is there), and
searching here involves, as we average over all possible orders of
presentation of the items and thus positions of the search item in the
sequence, $(k+1)/2$ probes.

The value of k depends upon the particular choice of keys. Each

130

of the $K-1$ items left (excluding the search item) has a chance of $1/N$ of being in position h. Thus the expected or average value of k is

1+mean of binomial distribution with $K-1$ trials, prob-

ability $\dfrac{1}{N} = 1 + \dfrac{K-1}{N}$.

Thus

E = expected number of probes

$$= \left(1 + \frac{K-1}{N} + 1\right)\Big/2 = 1 + \frac{K-1}{2N}.$$

We have seen a very simple analysis of hash tables using chaining. For hash tables where rehashing is used to resolve collisions, the analysis is considerably more tricky, since the sequences of items resulting from the resolution of collisions become joined to each other. For linear rehashing, the expected number of probes can be shown to be approximately

$$\frac{1 - \dfrac{x}{2}}{1 - \alpha}.$$

The analysis of this is too complex for consideration here (the interested reader should refer to the paper by Shay and Spruth, 'Analysis of a file addressing method', *Communications A.C.M.*, vol. 5 (August 1962), pp. 459–62, for a full analysis). Instead, we will make an approximate analysis in order to establish how good we might expect rehashing to be.

Let us make a simple assumption about the rehashing operation: let us assume that the combined operations of hashing and rehashing leads to a uniform distribution of items among the slots (roughly, each rehash operation would have to generate an address independently of any history or other keys in the table, uniformly distributing its addresses among the remaining slots). This means that when we analyse rehashing we can at any point consider M slots out of the N, containing J items, and say that the probability that a particular slot is occupied is just J/M, independently of the particular M slots. Now this assumption about independence corresponds to no **real** rehashing function, though it is often thought to correspond to the random rehash method. This correspondence would only be correct if the pseudo-random number generator selected was dependent upon the particular key, thus having a rehashing function which was an extension of the combination of the double hash method and random rehashing! Nevertheless, the result based upon this assumption is informative, and given in the following theorem.

THEOREM 4.3. With a hash table of K entries in N slots, using the independent rehash (discussed above) to resolve collisions, the expected number of key accesses or probes required to locate an item on lookup is approximately

$$E = - \left(\frac{1}{\alpha}\right) \log_e(1-\alpha), \quad \text{where} \quad \alpha = \frac{K}{N}.$$

Proof. We note that the number of probes required to lookup an item is exactly the same as the number of probes required to insert the item into the table in the first place. So let us calculate how many probes are required to insert a new item when there are already k items in the table. This will give a result $A(k)$, and to find E we will the need to sum $A(k)$ from 0 to $K-1$ and divide by K to find the average.

Consider inserting the $(k+1)th$ item into the table: let L be the number of probes required.

$$A(k) = \text{Expected value of } L = \sum_{j=1}^{k+1} j \cdot \Pr(L=j)$$

Now $\quad \Pr(L = j) = \Pr(L \geq j) - \Pr(L \geq j+1)$

and $\quad \Pr(L \geq 1) = 1$ because certain to put item somwhere

$\Pr(L \geq 2) = $ probability that have collision on first rehash

$\quad = \dfrac{k}{N}$ (see discussion just before theorem)

$\Pr(L \geq 3) = $ probability that collision on first and second

$\quad = \dfrac{k}{N} \cdot \dfrac{k-1}{N-1}$ **by independence**

. . .

$$\Pr(L \geq k+1) = \frac{k(k-1) \ldots 1}{N(N-1) \ldots (N-k+1)}$$

$\Pr(L \geq k+2) = 0$ because must have made it by this point.

Hence,

$$A(k) = \sum_{j=1}^{k+1} j[\Pr(L \geq j) - \Pr(L \geq j+1)] = \sum_{j=1}^{k+1} \Pr(L \geq j)$$

$$= 1 + \frac{k}{N} + \frac{k(k-1)}{N(N-1)} + \ldots + \frac{k(k-1)(k-2)\ldots 1}{N(N-1)\ldots(N-k+1)}$$

$$= 1 + \frac{k}{N-k+1} \text{ by induction on } k$$

$$= \frac{1}{1 - \dfrac{k}{N+1}}$$

Note. The induction is a little tricky: write $N = M+k$, then fix M, and then induce on k. It then goes through quite readily.

Now
$$E = \frac{1}{K} \sum_{k=0}^{K-1} A(k)$$

$$= \frac{1}{K} \sum_{k=0}^{K} \frac{1}{1 - \dfrac{k}{N+1}}$$

$$\leq \frac{1}{K} \int_0^K \frac{1}{1 - \dfrac{k}{N+1}} dk = \frac{N}{K} \int_0^{K/N} \frac{1}{1 - \dfrac{k}{N+1}} d\left(\frac{k}{N}\right)$$

$$\leq \frac{1}{\alpha} \int_0^{\alpha} \frac{1}{1-x} dx \text{ writing } x = \frac{k}{N}, \alpha = \frac{K}{N}, \text{ and using } \frac{k}{N+1}$$
$$< x < 1$$

$$= -\frac{1}{\alpha} \log_e(1-\alpha)$$

Table 4.4 shows the three formulae for hash tables evaluated for various values of α. Notice that for rehashing, we are limited to $\alpha \leq 1$ but for chaining can actually have $\alpha > 1$ with quite acceptable efficiency.

Hash tables have shown us how the controlled use of extra storage can lead to a great improvement in efficiency. We conclude that for large tables we should always use hash tables, but with a proviso. The effectiveness of hash tables rests upon our ability to find an effective initial hash function and thus overcome primary clustering, and in rehashing also demands that we find an effective rehash function. The efficiency is critically dependent upon the initial hash uniformly distributing the actual keys among the storage slots: where this cannot be achieved, or where the worst case where all keys hash to the same slot (and thus in most forms of hashing the method degenerates into a sequential table), cannot be tolerated, other table methods may be more appropriate.

In summary we conclude:

for medium to large table use hash tables unless special requirements demand other methods. Use either chained resolution of collisions, or rehashing with double hashing as the preferred method. A multi-level decoding form of hashing should always be considered.

Packing density $K/N = \alpha$	Expected number of probes		
	Chaining $1 + \alpha/2$	Linear rehash $(1 - \alpha/2)/(1 - \alpha)$	Independent rehash $-1/\alpha \log(1 - \alpha)$
0·1	1·05	1·06	1·05
0·5	1·25	1·50	1·39
0·75	1·38	2·50	1·83
0·9	1·45	5·50	2·56
0·99	1·50	50·5	4·65
1·5	1·75	—	—
2·0	2·00	—	—
5·0	3·5	—	—

Table 4.4. Hash tables: number of probes required on looking up a random item.

4.1.4 General considerations and over-all assessment

Table 4.5 summarises the efficiencies of the various table methods that we have studied. Figures for both insertions and lookups have

Table size K

Method	Operation	10	20	50	100	200	500	1,000	Formula
Sequential vector sorted	Insert.	11·9	21·9	52·0	102	202	502	1,002	$K+1+\dfrac{K}{K+1}$
	Lookup	5·5	10·5	25·5	55·5	101	251	501	$\dfrac{K+1}{2}$
Comparison tree logsearch	Insert.	9·3	15·4	31·7	57·7	108	264	511	$\log_2(K+1)+\dfrac{K}{2}+1$
	Lookup	2·7	3·6	4·8	5·7	7·0	8·0	9·0	$\dfrac{K+1}{K}\log_2(K+1)-1$
Comparison tree. Chained	Insert	5·7	7·2	8·9	10·3	11·7	13·6	15·0	$1\!\cdot\!4\log_2(K+1)+1$
	Lookup	4·2	5·5	7·1	8·4	10·2	11·6	13·0	$1\!\cdot\!4\dfrac{K+1}{K}\log_2(K+1)-1$
Hash. $\alpha = 0\!\cdot\!5$ chained overflow	Insert.	2·25	2·25	2·25	2·25	2·25	2·25	2·25	$2+\alpha/2$
	Lookup	1·25	2·25	1·25	1·25	1·25	1·25	1·25	$1+\alpha/2$

Table 4.5. Comparison of internal table methods. In the table the number of key accesses is shown for various sizes of table. Only the operations of insertion and lookup are given. Deletion is similar to insertion: in both cases with chaining there is a significant overhead in pointer manipulations. The hash table figures disguise the possible significant cost of hashing. With these qualifications in mind we see from the table that all methods are comparable for small tables while for large tables hashing is best. However, hashing relies on assumptions about key distributions and where these are inappropriate, one of the tree methods (possibly chained comparison with restructuring) could be preferable.

135

been given, to contrast the requirements of tables which are fixed, or almost fixed, and those which are dynamically changing due to deletions and insertions. A rough guide to the best buy is given in the table: which method one chooses depends upon ease of programming, as well as speed and storage requirements. Sequential tables would be used for most small tables, on the grounds of easy programming, but could even be used for large tables if the table is only occasionally used within the program. In going to more complex table methods, not only must we bear in mind the mix of operations, lookups versus changes, but also considerations of the relative sizes of keys, entries, and pointers.

Keys can be quite complicated, and accessing and comparing them can be a comparatively length process (e.g., where the keys are strings). This then makes other operations, notably pointer manipulations, considerably more attractive in terms of speed. In general pointers will occupy less storage than keys, which will occupy less storage than entries. This makes the extra storage used for pointers a comparatively small overhead.

This comparative cheapness of pointers not only makes chaining methods more attractive than one might otherwise have thought, but also suggests that we use more pointers. Let us store a table of pointers to items, rather than the items themselves, storing the items themselves (or perhaps just the entries) in order of arrival in a simple sequential unsorted vector table. The table of pointers could be structured for efficiency, with the advantage that any movement of items (if the method demands this) in the efficient table becomes simply the movement of pointers. We also gain two paths of access to our data—either via the fast table of pointers, or sequentially through the items in the order of arrival. We shall see variations on this idea later when we consider files where multiple paths of access are required.

4.2 External files

So far we have studied simple files stored entirely within the random access core memory of the computer. How do things change if the files are held on an external medium? Here we are severely constrained in the way in which we organise our files, constrained by the inherent structure of the storage medium. The extreme case is magnetic tape (and also paper tape), for here we can only move forwards or backwards along the tape to access from one data item to an adjacent data item. We are constrained to **serial** or **sequential** access, and are thus limited to precisely the basic techniques of sequential tables, studied in section 4.1.1. We shall only study magnetic tape because it is an extreme case, and is a long established external storage medium. With discs, the inherent structure of the medium is more complex and less well established: for more detailed consideration of discs and drums and related storage media, the reader should refer, for example, to the books by Knuth, or Lefkovitz, or Martin.

Suppose that we have a file held on magnetic tape, and we are given a key k and wish to find the item in the file having this key. If the file is unsorted, then we would have to start at one end of the file (i.e., magnetic tape) and search on the average half-way in order to find the item. If the item was not in the file, then we would have to search the whole file to find that it was not there. Now if the file was sorted, what do we gain? We could start at any point, compare the search key with the item at the position within the file that we find ourselves, and search either up or down the file depending upon the result of the comparison. We search until a key match is obtained, or we find that we have gone too far and can conclude that the item is not in the file. In either case, with a sorted file starting at a random point in the file and searching for a random key, we search on the average through one third of the file. Thus search is proportional to N the length of the file, and since N could typically be 100,000 records, this is disastrous. We must think of some other approach, the answer being to arrange that the search keys are anything but independent of each other! We collect many search requests together in a **batch**, sort these, and then process them within a **file merge** operation as explained in the following subsection.

It is not always possible to batch the requests for a file search, and a sensible strategy where this is the case is to sort the file so that the most frequently required items occur at the beginning of the file—as was suggested for sequential tables, section 4.1.1. A typical situation where this may be the case is in program libraries attached to link loaders.

4.2.1 Batching and merging

When processing a single operation on a sequential file independently of any other operations, we have little advantage in arranging that the file is sorted. However, if many separate operations upon a file are collected together or batched, then sorting can be very useful. Let us call any operation on a single item of data within the file a **transaction**, and the collection of transactions the **transaction file**. The **master file**, on which these transactions will take place, we shall call the **source file**. We shall suppose that the source file is sorted by the key of the data items, and suppose that we have sorted the transactions file by the same key. We shall see methods for actually performing this sorting in the next chapter, Chapter 5.

Let us denote the items or records of the source file by

$$S = \{s_1, s_2, ..., s_N \text{ where } s_i < s_j \text{ if } i < j\}.$$

Similarly let us denote the transactions file by

$$T = \{t_1, t_2, ..., t_M \text{ where } t_i < t_j \text{ if } i < j\}.$$

We have loosely written $s_i < s_j$ to mean that the keys are in the specified order, and will similarly denote comparisons between keys of records in the two separate files.

We now perform the transactions in a batch, starting at t_1, finding the matching record of S, make the transaction indicated, step on to t_2, and search forward through S to find a match, make the next transaction, and so on. Because S and T are sorted by the same key, we only need pass once through the source file in order to execute all the transactions, and that means a considerable saving! We shall call this method of stepping through the two files in parallel a (generalised) **file merge**. It is basic technique of digital computing.

In general the transactions can alter the original file by updating some of the information, or by inserting new items, or by deleting old items. No attempt is made to alter the source file directly. Instead, the file is copied onto a new magnetic tape, the alterations being made during the passage through the computer. This creates a new file, called the **object file**, see Fig. 4.14. Both the source file and the object file are essentially the same files, but are of different **generations**, and the way that files are given names within computing operating systems brings out this fact. Often, for security reasons, several generations of a file are stored, in case of accidents, a wrong transaction, or some computer hardware error. The object file is not necessary if the transactions do not change the file. Note that the order of presentation of the transactions could be important, since we might, for example, change the information in a record, and then refer to that record expecting the newer information. This situation is alright providing only that the sorting method for transactions preserves the order of presentation if the keys are identical.

SOURCE FILE   TRANSACTIONS   OBJECT FILE
                   FILE

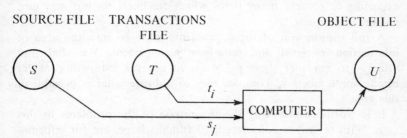

Fig. 4.13. Diagram illustrating a merge process, the direction of information flow from source and transactions files through the computer to the object file

Merging provides the basic method for off-line editing—a file of insertions, deletions, and updates is merged with another file to produce a new edited version of that file (see Chapter 3 for further details about editors). Merging also provides us with a basic technique for sorting. If we assume that all the transactions are insertions then we start with two files, both of which are sorted, and by merging them, obtain a combined file which is also sorted. We shall see a lot more of merging in Chapter 5, where sorting is studied in detail.

The techniques discussed above have referred to simple files with no hierarchical structure of subfiles, subsubfiles, etc. Of course such hierarchical files can be sorted, by sorting at each level (lexicographically) as was seen in Fig. 4.1. File merging is also possible, with transactions capable of occurring at any level.

.3 Complex files

The files that we have seen so far contain many individual items related to each other within a hierarchical tree structure. The items

139

each have a single key through which we can refer to and access the items. However, many problems are considerably more complex than this. The relationships between the items may be graph-like rather than tree-like, and there may be many different kinds of item within the file. Each item may have many separate potential keys or **attributes,** and we may wish to access the data through any of these attributes, or any combinations of these attributes. We may wish to retrieve information (i.e., items) from the file with imprecise requests, expecting to retrieve many items which are likely to, but may not, answer the request.

A full exploration of these problems takes us into the area of **information retrieval** and **data-base management.** We shall not attempt to consider these problems in general, but will consider briefly some facets of complex files to indicate what is possible in this area.

It is worth emphasising the magnitude of the problems in this area. With tables we considered 1,000 items large, but for information systems, 1,000 items is small and files may often contain in excess of a million items! Structuring for efficiency is critical.

Let us consider a small example, a telephone directory. Normally the information in the directory is accessed through the telephone subscriber's name, from which either his telephone number or address may be obtained. However, exceptionally we may want to find out who is the subscriber for a particular number, or whether there is a telephone at a particular address. There are three attributes or potential keys. The subscriber's name is the most important, so we will call it the **primary key,** while the other attributes form **secondary keys.** Now a given attribute may not uniquely identify a single item—in the example, given an address, there may be several numbers and several subscribers associated with that address. Whenever we use an attribute as a key to the file, and access the file searching for a particular attribute value, we shall assume that we retrieve **all** items with the particular attribute value. All our table methods of section 4.1 could be adjusted to ensure this.

If we have structured the file for access via the primary key, and we wish to access the file through some secondary key, we would have to conduct an exhaustive search, treating the file as the simplest form of sequential file, unless we in some way imposed extra structure to aid access via this secondary key. The simplest way to do this would be to **invert** the file and produce a second file in which the access key is the secondary key in which we are interested. This would then be an **inverted file**. We would not necessarily have to duplicate all our information, since our entries in the inverted file could be some form of pointer to the primary data stored in the original file. The access path for the secondary key need not be as efficient as that for the primary key if the secondary access paths are not used so often. Where there are more than one secondary key, we would have an inverted file for each secondary key.

Where there are many keys, each considered of equal importance, we would like each key to have the same mode of access. This could be set up using tables of pointers, one table for each key or attribute, applying the techniques of section 4.1. This could mean storing the data separately from the tables accessing the data, but this is not necessary. To give some idea of how the paths of access and the data can be combined, let us consider an example, the telephone directory example for the internal telephone directory of some fictitious organisation. A sequence of possible file designs is given in Fig. 4.14. Let us start with a simple design, considering only the primary key used in a chained sorted sequential table, as in Fig. 4.14(a). Now consider number as a secondary key, and add pointers to chain access paths via numbers also as a chained sorted sequential table. This leads to a multi-linked structure, as in Fig. 4.14(b). Sequential access is not critical to the design, and we could arrange that access by name was faster, using a decoding tree, as in Fig. 4.14(c). Numbers, and addresses could be treated in like manner. The design of Fig. 4.14(c) has the disadvantage that it is unidirectional. Having found JONES, for example, we could not simply move on down the name sequence from J to K unless we had anticipated this and left suitable pointers from where we could pick up the search. The extra flexibility is easily gained by using rings to give the bidirectionality, at the same time placing an extra label field in the records in order to mark the position where passage round a ring leads to a change in level in the tree (we have seen these ideas before in Chapter 2). Making these changes, and at the same time giving a decoding tree access to numbers, leads to the design in Fig. 4.14(d).

This example has served to show some of the possibilities and complexities that arise when we consider several different paths of access to the data in a file. Real problems would be much richer,

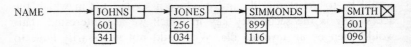

(a) Sequential access by NAME only.

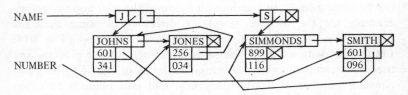

(b) Sequential access by NAME and NUMBER.

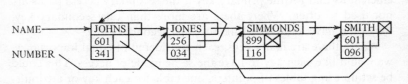

(c) Decoding tree access by NAME, sequential access by NUMBER.

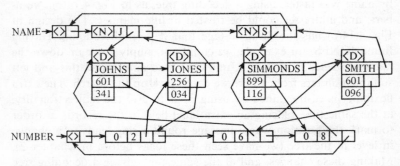

(d) Using rings to provide bidirectionality, with decoding trees for both NAME and NUMBER.

Fig. 4.14. *File designs for the internal telephone directory of a fictitious organisation. In the data records the first data field is the NAME, the second is the telephone NUMBER, and the third is the ROOM number.*

having many more paths of access with many more levels in the 'trees', as well as having items of many different types related in a graph-like manner.

The separate sections of storage structure that we have set up for access to the data are often called **indexes**, and we talk of primary indexes and secondary indexes. Often the questions about the data will involve ranges of values of keys. In this case it is useful if the indexes involved use the sort order of the keys. Thus binary tree techniques, or an order preserving hash table, would be useful. For large sets of data stored on discs, the resulting index will be an n-ary tree, perhaps in several levels. One variation of this is known as **indexed sequential,** another variation as a **B-tree.**

Our access requirements can be yet more complicated. We could be given a logical combination of attribute values, only insisting that some are satisfied. Another variation would wish to look for all data 'similar to' some given data. A typical application where these more complex requirements occur is in library information retrieval systems.

For further reading in this important branch of computing, the books by Henley, Lefkovitz, Date, Knuth, and Salton all cover various aspects of the design of large files for complex information systems.

4 Exercises

1 Fill in the missing details for Routines 4.3, 4.4, and 4.7.

2 Formulate fully the hash table routines with rehashing to resolve collisions, maintaining the items **sorted** within the vector of records, ready for an ordered printout. See section 4.1.3.2 for hints on how to do this.

3 For all the table methods of section 4.1, formulate combined insert/ update routines so that an incoming item (K,E) either updates the entry of item with key K if it exists, or inserts a new item into the table if key K is not yet in the table.

4.4.4 Choose two sample table problems, say one where the keys are a simple integer numbers, with integer entries, and one where the keys are alphabetic strings and the entries occupy several words of storage, and compare the speed of operation of all the many table techniques of section 4.1. Do this experimentally, by programming the various methods in some suitable language. Having programmed the methods, and tested them thoroughly, then measure the time taken to perform one of each operation at various table sizes—for example, the time taken to insert one item into a table that already contains 500 items. Be sure to obtain an average time, averaged over all possible selections of search key, all possible orders of arrival of the data into the table. Part of this averaging will be achieved in overcoming the difficulties of obtaining times at all, and part of the averaging will require repeated experiments using different test data. Compare where possible your results with the theoretical results.

Note that the time taken for the computer to perform a task can be tricky to measure, and calls for laboratory methods which would not normally be taught within a course on computing science. Computers work very fast, and usually contain within them some form of clock which can be used to make the timing measurements. Part of your program becomes an experimenter which times the table operations under investigation. Now the computer's internal clock is often very coarse, measuring only to the nearest second if you are unlucky, or perhaps to the nearest millisecond if you are lucky. In a multi-programming environment make sure that you obtain your own central processor time, and not elapsed time. Most of the table operations will take less than a millisecond, so if you just measure how long it takes to perform, say, one insertion, you will most often get an answer of 0·000 seconds! The answer is to time the execution of many operations, choosing a random selection of keys, and then take the average of these. You might need to time as many as 1,000 operations in order to obtain sensible times. In order to make sure that it is the operation which is taking the time, and not 'overheads' such as the generation of the test data, we would then need to time the operations once where we do nothing in the operation, and then subtract this overhead time to obtain the time actually spent on the operation. The methods discussed so far are perfectly adequate for lookup and update and printout operations, but insertions and deletions change the size of the table, so that if we repeat the operation we do not obtain an average for a fixed size of table. For insertions and deletions we can instead use a differential technique, and plot curves of total time to form up a table (time taken against size of table) using insertions, or time to diminish a table using deletions, when the derivative of the curve at particular points will provide the times that we are after. Timing deletions in hash–rehash tables will be exceptional, and difficult.

.5 Formulate a generalised file merge following the principles discussed in Section 4.2.1. Arrange that insertions can be immediately followed by other transactions on this new record, including the possible deletion of the new record.

.6 Formulate a table algorithm based on trees (as in Section 4.1.2), but which partitions the set of keys into subsets of keys close to some central key. Program this with strings as keys, using string similarity of Exercise 3.4.2. [Hint: refer to book by Salton.]

.7 An important part of an assembler, and a compiler, is the formation of the user symbol table. The following is an abstraction of the problem, and contains all the essential ingredients. Write a program to perform the task specified there. If you are familiar with an assembler language, modify the problem below to make your program perform the 'first pass' of a two pass assembler.

The problem data is a (very long) string of characters: letters, spaces, colons, and newlines (or carriage return, line feed characters). The sequence of symbols between newline characters we will talk of as being on the same line (naturally) and we will number the lines starting from line 1 being the characters before the first newline symbol, and numbering consecutively from there. Any string of letters bounded by a space, colon, or newline at both ends, forms a word, and we shall term the symbols space, colon, and newline 'separators' because they separate words from each other. Any particular word may occur many times in the data string. Some words occur immediately followed by a colon (and this is the only position in which colons do occur); this is called a defining occurrence of the word, the value given to the definition of the word being the number of the line on which the defining occurrence happens.

The task is to scan the data stream once, keeping track of the line

145

number, segmenting the string into words using the separators, and identifying defining occurrences of words as they are segmented from the string. A table of all the words found to date is maintained: the word is the key, and the definition (line number) is the entry. As each word is isolated from the data string, it is checked against the table, and inserted if not there, either with its definition if the occurrence was defining, or with the value undefined (numeral 0) if the occurrence was not defining. If the word is already in the table, then its entry is updated if the occurrence is defining, and an error-message is given if the update leads to a redefinition of the word. At the end of the data string, marked by an end-of-file character, the table is printed out with the words arranged in alphabetical order.

For example, the data string

> ONE TWO: THREE ONE: (newline)
> FOUR: THREE ONE: (newline)
> ONE: ONE TWO FOUR THREE (end-of-file)

where the control characters newline and end-of-file have been shown in brackets to indicate a single character, and the display of the data string on three lines is only for clarity of presentation, leads to the output

> ERROR—ONE IS REDEFINED ON LINE 2
> ERROR—ONE IS REDEFINED ON LINE 3

TABLE IS

FOUR	2
ONE	3
THREE	0
TWO	1

4.4.8 Select one of the programming languages that you use frequently, and program a macro-preprocessor for this language. Macros (see section 2.2, and the books by Gries, and Barron, for further information) are an aid to programming which allows you to use a form of shorthand that looks very like subroutine calls, with these shorthands being detected during a pass prior to any assembly or compilation, and a fully detailed expansion of the shorthand being inserted to replace the 'call' of the macro. Macros have to be defined prior to their first call, and at their simplest would not be allowed to further

146

call other macros, though this and even macro recursion is possible. For your macro-preprocessor make macro-calls take the same format as subroutine calls, including functions, and arguments, inventing your own conventions for macro-definitions and the way arguments are substituted into the macro-body.

The program that you write will rely on good string handling ability (Chapter 3) and table techniques (section 4.1), though the table method could be slow if not many macros are likely to be defined. Note that a macro table has very different characteristics from the other tables in assemblers and compilers in that it contains only a few, but bulky, items.

5 Sorting

In this chapter we shall study another important class of computing problems, that of sorting files, of arranging collections of items of data into order.

While it is obvious what is meant by sorting, let us abstract some precise statement of what is required within a sorting process. We are given a set containing N items. This set is totally ordered, in that for any two items a and b in the set there holds an ordering relation, with either $a < b$ or $a = b$ or $b < a$. We must obtain an indexing on the set of items (that is, number them from 1 to N) such that $i < j$ implies $a_i \leq a_j$ for all i and j from 1 to N. In concrete terms, the indexing corresponds to the ordinal position of the item within a sequential file, or the offset of the item within a vector of storage. Usually in sorting we start off with the set indexed in some arbitrary manner, and the production of the sorted set involves permuting the set of items until the indexing of the set and the ordering of the set agree. We shall see a great variety of methods for sorting, with different areas of applicability, and will analyse their effectiveness in terms of the size of the set N, and in terms of ease of programming.

As we have argued previously, in section 4.2, a prime reason for sorting is to assist in the orderly management of large quantities of data. Sorting was important for sequential files where merging techniques were used for processing the files. While this is the major reason for sorting, one must note that with the advance of technology to storage media where there is no constraint requiring sequential access, the importance of sorting within file management diminishes.

There are three further reasons for sorting. One reason lies in the orderly presentation of data for human consumption, and that is a reason which will continue in importance. We have already seen this factor when studying tables, where we considered one important

148

function of tables is their printout in order of ascending key. A second reason for sorting arises in the analysis of experimental data by numerical processes, where the numerical computations require the data in specific orders which may not coincide with the order in which the data was gathered. The third reason for sorting arises in the statistical analysis of data, using order statistics. An order statistic or percentile, $x(p)$, is that data value which has $p\%$ of the data values greater than it. Acquiring order statistics means arranging all the items of data into two subsets, those that are large together, and those that are small together, such that the correct proportion of the items fall in the two sets. This does not mean we must fully sort the data, and by partially sorting we can find the required order statistic with considerable saving of effort. We shall see one method for this partial sorting while studying techniques for completely sorting the data.

As in the previous chapters, we shall need to consider two varieties of problem, internal and external. When the data to be sorted fits entirely within the computer primary storage we are concerned with **internal sorting**, while when the data is too numerous for internal storage and requires external storage, we are concerned with **external sorting**. As we shall see, external sorts rely on internal sorts at some point in their execution, and so it is to internal sorts that we shall first turn.

In all cases of sorting, it is not the complete item of data which is used in determining the ordering, but only a part of the item, called the **sort key**. The key could be alphanumeric strings, or numbers, or some other possibility. We shall be rather loose in the way we express our algorithms, acting as if the item consisted purely of the key, and as if the key were numeric. Further, where necessary we will make the assumption that an item occupies a single slot of storage and thus, for example, when stepping from one item to the next in internal storage, we will simply need to step on by one. Hence in part we shall avoid storage level details, and yet on the other hand must consider methods of storage since we shall often be concerned with trees, and must decide how to store these. Thus the methods will be presented as routines, though there will be some labour involved in translating from the routines as here presented to a program for a particular problem.

5.1 Internal sorting

For internal sorting we have no constraints concerning the structures that we can use in solving our problem. We shall see many methods that exploit tree structures in order to achieve an efficient sort. Usually the trees will appear implicitly either buried within the algorithm and its control structure, or with the tree edges defined by address arithmetic. Exceptionally the tree will be explicit through chaining.

We shall be concerned with efficiency, both of storage and of time, as well as with ease of programming. Ease of programming includes ease of understanding the method to be used, for it is essential to understand a method to successfully program it.

Let us consider storage requirements. As indicated previously, we shall suppose that there are N items to be sorted, and will suppose that each item occupies one storage slot, and thus require at least N storage slots for our sorting process. All algorithms will require extra storage for their instructions, and certain control values, but may also require additional storage because of the nature of the method used. This additional storage may be fixed, but may vary with N. Some algorithms require as many as $4N$ extra storage slots, while others require no extra storage, other than that required by the algorithm and a fixed set of control variables. Results on storage must be treated with caution, because we have assumed that all items occupy a single slot, but as discussed in section 4.1.4 this is not necessarily the case. Often the extra storage is for pointers, and as we have argued, these might be comparatively cheap. Also some algorithms require an input buffer area, or an output buffer area, and if an external medium could be used directly in this buffering capacity, we could save this extra storage. Cases where this is possible will be indicated as they are examined.

The speed of an algorithm is a function of many factors We shall obtain a simple assessment by considering the number of comparisons. Simple minded algorithms require of order N^2 comparisons (though I have even come across methods that require of order N^3 comparisons!) while the best require only of order $N \log_2 N$ comparisons, with one anomalous method, address calculation sort which is related to hash tables, requiring only of order N. We ought to expect the $N \log_2 N$ figure, because if we have N items altogether, there are $N!$ (N factorial) possible orders in which the items could be presented to the computer, and in effect sorting means identifying which of the $N!$ possible initial arrangements is the one presented. Finding out which particular arrangement has been presented can be done by asking questions of a YES/NO binary nature, requiring altogether $\log_2(N!) \approx N \log_2 N$ questions to bisect the set of possibilities to a set of a single element. In information theory terminology, we say that there are $N \log_2 N$ bits of information present.

For analysis purposes we will suppose that no two items have equal keys, but the algorithms themselves must cope with equal keys. Items with equal keys start with one item having a smaller index than the other, and after sorting this should still be the case. Sorting methods that guarantee this are called **stable**. Stability is desirable for merge processing (see section 4.2.1), so that the first transaction presented for processing is still done first, even after sorting. Stable sort methods will be indicated as they are studied.

.1 Internal sorting strategies

There are four important approaches to internal sorting, which motivate the algorithms produced. These are:

(i) SELECTION: the largest (or smallest) item in the set is selected, placed in the correct position ready for output, and then the remaining items are treated similarly.

(ii) INSERTION: the items are handled one at a time in any order, and the sorted set is built up by successively inserting each new item into its correct position within the set so far.

(iii) DISTRIBUTION: the items are distributed into subsets so that all the small items lie in one subset, all the large items lie in another subset, with intermediate subsets containing intermediate items.

(iv) MERGE: sorted subsets are combined into larger sorted subsets using merging to effect the combination.

In fact, (i) and (ii) can be regarded as special cases of (iii) and (iv) respectively, but they have special techniques associated with them and will be treated separately.

There is a fifth approach that we could have considered. This implicitly measures the degree of sorting (for example, as the total number of pairs of items out of order) and then swaps item pairs so that at each swap the degree of sort is improved. The methods obtained from this approach often coincide with methods in the other four categories, with one significant exception, Shell sort. This method however, is not as efficient as other methods and will be considered only within the exercises. Where the methods that we consider also fall into this fifth category of sort-improvement, we shall indicate the fact.

5.1.2 Selection sorts

These sorting methods work by building up the sorted set by selecting at each cycle the smallest (or largest) element remaining in the **input set**, and then appending this to the appropriate end of the sorted **output set**. In presenting the various ideas based on these ideas, we shall invariably select the smallest, but of course could equally well have selected the largest.

In practice, after selecting an item from the input set, it could be output directly, thus making the storage of the output set external rather than internal. In the routines that we study the output set will be taken as internal, but the extra storage bound up with this can be ignored in many applications. All selection sort methods can be programmed so that they are stable; when two items appear with identical key, the one that was presented first is selected first. This has been done in all the routines that are presented below.

The general form of the method is shown in the following algorithm.

ALGORITHM 5.1. *Selection sort, general method*
1. $k \leftarrow 1$; while $k \leq N$ do
2. $_1[$ Select the smallest item from the input set;
3. Transfer this element to the position just after the previous element placed in the output set;
4. Delete that element from the input set;
5. $k \leftarrow k+1;]_1$
6. **Exit.**

All concrete realisations of selection sorts take the form of Algorithm 5.1, though there are great differences with respect to the methods for storage of the input and output sets, and the method for selecting the smallest element of the input set. The very simplest idea is to set aside two distinct areas $a[1:N]$ and $b[1:N]$ for the input and output sets respectively, to select the smallest element by a simple scan of vector $a[1:N]$, transfering this to the correct position $b[k]$ of the output set, and then deleting the selected item from $a[1:N]$ by setting the element to $+\infty$ or some very large value. This is not a method one would ever use in practice.

Now the input and output sets can be made to share the same storage area, $a[1:N]$, with the input set being $a[k:N]$ and the output set being $a[1:k-1]$ with the transfer of item, step 3, achieved in the combined placing of the smallest item in $a[k]$ and the incrementing of k. There are many more or less equivalent methods for selecting the smallest item of a set. The simplest method would scan the set, keeping a record of the smallest so far, extracting this at the end of the scan. There are $N-1$ cycles of selection, the first involving $N-1$ comparisons, the second involving $N-2$ comparisons, and so on, giving a total of $N(N-1)/2$ comparisons, that is, of order N^2 comparisons. Storage is the minimum possible, N storage slots for data plus a constant extra storage for algorithm and its control.

An alternative method of selection is based on the bubbling idea we saw first in Sequential tables. Instead of maintaining a pointer m to the smallest so far, or maintaining a copy of it, or swapping it into the correct position each time a new candidate smallest is found, we sweep through the vector of items carrying with us the smallest so far, leaving behind the discarded candidates as they are rejected. This method allows for early termination by detecting that the remaining data is already in order. This is discovered when our bubble sweep no longer carries anything with it.

ROUTINE 5.2. *Bubble selection sort*
1. $k \leftarrow 1$; flag $\leftarrow$ **true**; while $k < N$ and flag **do**
2. $\quad_1[\cancel{c}$ select the smallest item in input set $a[k:N]$ $\cancel{c}$
$\qquad j \leftarrow N$; flag $\leftarrow$ **false**;
$\qquad$ **while** $j > k$ **do**
$\qquad\quad_2[$**if** $a[j] < a[j-1]$
$\qquad\qquad$ **then**$_3[\cancel{c}$ exchange and set flag $\cancel{c}$ flag $\leftarrow$ **true**;
$\qquad\qquad\qquad$ temp$\leftarrow a[j]$; $a[j]\leftarrow a[j-1]$; $a[j-1]\leftarrow$ temp$;]_3$
$\qquad\qquad j \leftarrow j-1;]_2$

153

3.   ¢ decrease input set. No need to transfer the smallest
                       to the output set, since bubbling will already have
                       placed it there. If no bubbling occurred, flag is **false**
                       and cycle terminates. ¢

         $k \leftarrow k+1$;

    ]₁

4. **Exit.** ¢ sorted data in $a[1:N]$ ¢

If the data is sorted to start with, then this algorithm would stop
after the first cycle, having used only $N-1$ comparisons of keys.
However, if we assume that all initial arrangements are equally
likely, then it can be shown analytically that the number of comparisons is still of order N^2, and experimentation shows that the
extra effort involved in using the flag outweighs any advantage of
early termination, and in the end we are worse off! There is a general
lesson in that: doing extra work to save time can waste time. Bubble
selection is the only selection sort which is also sort-improving.

It should be noted that the three preceding routines could also be
programmed using chained storage, with the indexing being implicit
in the chained sequence. However, there is no advantage in this.
Indeed, we shall see that chaining is only exceptionally profitably
used within sorting routines.

So far the routines have had time efficiency of order N^2 comparisons, and that simply is not good enough. What can be done
about it? Clearly during the selection process we are wasting effort,
for in selecting the smallest item, we also find other small items only
to discard this knowledge later.

Let us consider another method for the selection of the smallest
element of a set. We arrange a tournament among the items in the
set, pairing them off to obtain a second round with $[N/2]$ elements,
the smaller of all the pairs. The winners are then paired off, a further
set of winners are found for the third round, and so on, as shown in
Fig. 5.1. To find the smallest element of the complete set still requires
$N-1$ comparisons, but observe what happens when we want to find
the second smallest. We remove the smallest from the tournament
by replacing it by $+\infty$ or some very large value that is guaranteed to
lose, and then we replay the tournament, but in practice only need
replay that part of the tournament in which the previous largest was
involved. This involves only at most $[\log_2 N]$ comparisons. This

means that for the complete sorting operation we require approximately $N-1+(N-1)\log_2 N$ comparisons. But the tournament sort idea is very tricky to program, and requires extra storage. The interested reader can consult an Algol-60 encoding of this method in a form called Treesort, as Algorithm 113 in the *Communications of the A.C.M.* (August 1962), p. 434. Fortunately this tournament sort has been completely superceded by a considerably more elegant and efficient method, called Treesort3 when it first appeared as *C.A.C.M.* Algorithm 245 (December 1964).

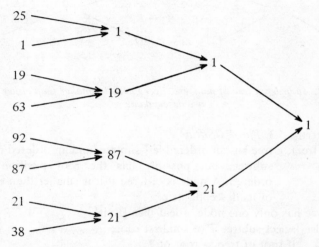

Fig. 5.1. A tournament of 8 numbers, to select the smallest. The winner is 1. When the 1 is deleted from the tournament and replaced by $+\infty$, the tournament can be replayed by replaying only the branches of the tree at the top of the diagram, to select 19 as winner. Selecting the first cycle winner takes 7 comparisons, while the selection of the second cycle winner only takes 3 comparisons between 25 and $+\infty$, 25 and 19, 19 and 21.

We can maintain the efficiency of Tournament sort without requiring the extra storage by recognising that the essential property of the tree within the tournament is that every node is smaller than either of its two descendants. Arranging a tree with this property, using the data, does *not* require values to be repeated, as can be seen in Fig. 5.2. This tree can be mechanically formed from the data, and then successive values taken from the top using a tree generalisation of the bubbling idea, due to Floyd, the originator of Treesort3. We shall call this method Siftup, after Floyd, and present the idea in the algorithm below. Siftup takes a tree which is almost ordered in the way required, but has the root possibly misplaced, and bubbles the misplaced value from the root towards the leaves, until the complete tree becomes ordered. The general idea is set out in the following algorithm.

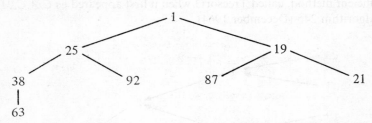

Fig. 5.2. An ordered tree of numbers. Every node is smaller than either of its two descendants.

ALGORITHM 5.3. *Floyd's Siftup*

Siftup(tree); ¢ tree has an ordered left-subtree, and an ordered right-subtree, but possibly has the root position not ordered. A node is ordered if it is smaller than either of its descendants ¢

1. **if** tree has only one node, a leaf **then** [**Exit**]
2.   **else**₁[select subtree T of smallest root;
3.   **if** root of tree $>$ root of T
4.   **then**₂[exchange roots of T and tree;
                 Siftup(T);]₂
5.   **Exit**.
       ]₁

Fig. 5.3 shows three stages in the execution of the algorithm siftup, where the root of the tree currently being examined by Siftup has been circled. In implementation the recursion in Siftup will be replaced by looping, as we shall see in Routines 5.4.

Now in order to sort a set of numbers, these numbers are formed into a binary tree, and then this binary tree is ordered using siftup repeatedly starting at the bottom of the tree and working upwards: leaves are trivially ordered, so we start with the lowest subtree that

156

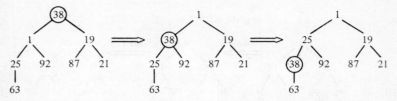

Fig. 5.3. The operation of Siftup. At the node circled, the two subtrees are ordered, but the node itself is misplaced, being (possibly) larger than one of its two descendants. Three stages are shown, as the misplaced node sifts from the root towards the leaves.

has more than one node, and progress successively higher and higher each time fully applying Siftup, until we reach the root. This is shown in Fig. 5.4. Note that at each application of Siftup, the tree supplied to it satisfies the partial ordered requirement of the algorithm, because we are working from the leaves towards the root. Having ordered the tree, the smallest item in the set must now be the item at the root: this can either be output directly to some external medium, or it can be stored internally. In either case some leaf is brought up to replace the root, the tree shrinks by one node, and

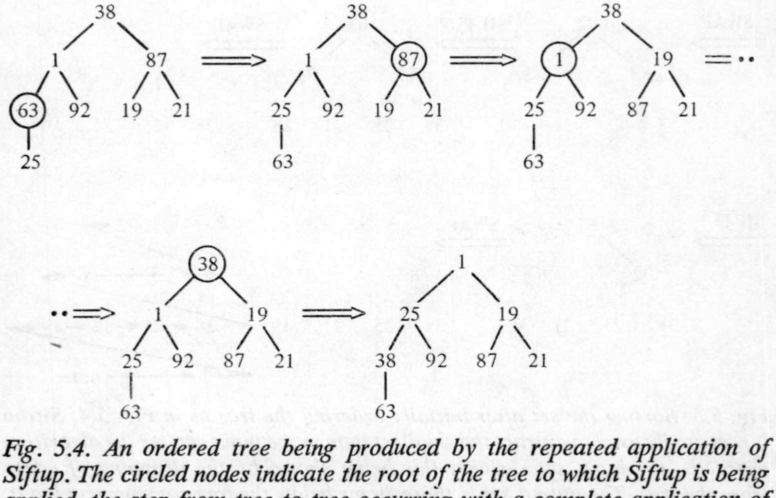

Fig. 5.4. An ordered tree being produced by the repeated application of Siftup. The circled nodes indicate the root of the tree to which Siftup is being applied, the step from tree to tree occurring with a complete application of Siftup, sifting the node as close to the leaf as it will go, to produce ordered subtrees.

157

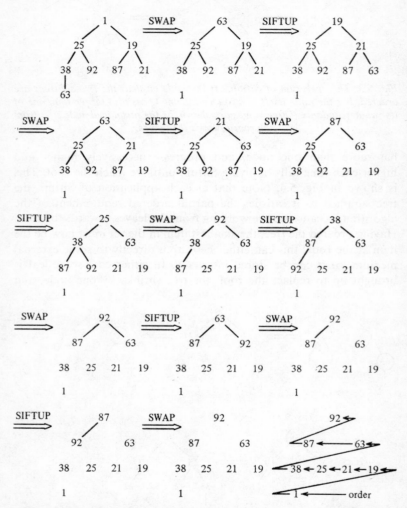

Fig. 5.5. Sorting the set after initially ordering the tree as in Fig. 5.4. Siftup is repeatedly used to extract the smallest item in the input set. As the algorithm proceeds, the input set shrinks, this being shown by the dropping of edges from the tree. The output set is those items below the tree not connected to it.

we are ready for another application of Siftup to extract the second smallest item of the set. We shall suppose that the selected item at the root is swapped with the leaf that replaces it. This is what actually does happen in Routines 5.4 below. Fig. 5.5 shows a complete sequence of Swaps and Siftups which take the input set after initial ordering of the tree (Fig. 5.4) through until the input set tree has been reduced to a single node, and the items are sorted, ordered in the sequence shown in the last portion of the figure.

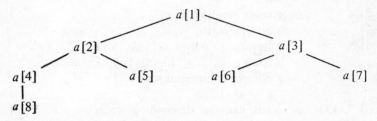

Fig. 5.6. Storage structure for the trees of Figs. 5.2 to 5.5. The items are stored in vector $a[1:N]$, with root at $a[1]$ and node $a[k]$ having edges to descendants $a[2k]$ and $a[2k+1]$.

We cannot, however, write down this method, informally presented with the aid of diagrams, unless we have a precise notation for binary trees. We might as well consider how we would represent the binary trees in storage, and present the method as a Routine in which the storage conventions have been fixed. There is only one reasonable way to store the binary tree, and that is by using a vector $a[1:N]$ with the edges of the tree implicit through address arithmetic, $a[k]$ having descendents $a[2k]$ and $a[2k+1]$, the root being $a[1]$. Vector storage has other advantages, as should become obvious from considering the Routines 5.4, and considering rival methods for storage of the tree. Fig. 5.6 shows a vector drawn out to emphasis the tree relationships, and thus show exactly how all the trees of Fig. 5.2 to 5.5 would be stored.

ROUTINES 5.4. *Treesort3*
Denote general subtrees in the vector $a[1:N]$ by a pair of integers (i,k) which specifies the subtree with root at $a[i]$ and no node extending beyond $a[k]$.

1. Treesort3(a,N); $\not\!c$ sorts data in random order in $a[1:N]$ into **descending** order also in $a[1:N]$ $\not\!c$
   1.1. $\not\!c$ order the left and right subtrees of data, $(2,N)$ and $(3,N)$, by starting at the lowest non-trivial subtree $(\lfloor N/2\rfloor,N)$ and continuing from there up the tree towards the root $\not\!c$
   $i \leftarrow \lfloor N/2\rfloor$; **while** $i \geq 2$ **do**
   1.2. $_1[\text{Siftup}(i,N); i \leftarrow i-1;]_1$
   1.3. $\not\!c$ repeatedly select the smallest and place in output set $\not\!c$
   $k \leftarrow N$; **while** $k > 1$ **do**
   1.4. $_2[\not\!c$ select smallest, in $a[1]$ $\not\!c$
   $\text{Siftup}(1,k);$
   1.5. $\not\!c$ transfer to output set $a[k:N]$ $\not\!c$
   $\text{temp} \leftarrow a[1]; a[1] \leftarrow a[k]; a[k] \leftarrow \text{temp};$
   1.6. $\not\!c$ remove from input set $\not\!c$
   $k \leftarrow k-1;]_2$
   1.7. **Exit.** $\not\!c$ sorted data in descending order in $a[1:N]$. To obtain in ascending order, change '$<$' to '$>$' in Siftup $\not\!c$
2. Siftup(i,k); $\not\!c$ orders subtree (i,k) given that it is partly ordered, with subsubtrees $(2i,k)$ and $(2i+1,k)$ ordered, and only the root possibly misplaced $\not\!c$
   2.1. $\not\!c$ take a copy of the root to be bubbled as close to the leaves as possible $\not\!c$
   $\text{copy} \leftarrow a[i];$
   2.2. **while** $\not\!c$ not at leaf $\not\!c$ $2*i \leq k$ **do**
   2.3. $_1[$**if** $\not\!c$ two descendents $\not\!c$ $2*i < k$
   2.4. **then**$_2[\not\!c$ select subtree of smallest root $\not\!c$
   if $a[2*i] < a[2*i+1]$
   2.5. **then** $[j \leftarrow 2*i;]$ **else**$[j \leftarrow 2*i+1]$
   $]_2$
   2.6. **else**$[j \leftarrow 2*i]$
   2.7. $\not\!c$ bubble root down if appropriate $\not\!c$
   if $a[j] < \text{copy}$
   2.8. **then**$[a[i] \leftarrow a[j]; i \leftarrow j]$ **else** $[a[i] \leftarrow \text{copy}; \textbf{Exit}];$
   $]_1$
   2.9. $\not\!c$ insert root value at correct position $\not\!c$
   $a[i] \leftarrow \text{copy};$
   2.10. **Exit.**

Note that this routine produces the sorted items in descending order: to change this we could select the largest rather than the smallest within Siftup, or change the conventions for edges. The routine has been expressed in this form because it **selects** the items in ascending order, and if output rather than swapping, we would obtain an ascending sequence on the external medium. We shall need this later in replacement sorting, where we will base the efficient replacement sort upon Treesort3.

The reader is encouraged to work through this algorithm on the example data (38,1,87,63,92,19,21,25) in the vector $a[1:8]$, using the tree of Fig. 5.6 to follow through the sequence of tree manipulations in Figs. 5.4 and 5.5.

Clearly Treesort3 uses no extra storage, and since a single application of Siftup in a tree on N nodes uses at most $2\lfloor \log_2 N \rfloor$ comparisons, we see that the number of comparisons in any execution of Treesort3 must be less than $2(N-1)\lfloor \log_2 N \rfloor$. Treesort3 is just about as good a sorting method as we have a right to expect. The programs themselves are relatively complex. Thus we conclude that we should only use Treesort3 where the extra effort is worth it, for sorting more than 10 or 20 items.

There are a variety of other selection sorts, notable among which is quadratic selection, where in effect a two level tree is arranged, a tournament in which $\sqrt{N}$ items are played against each other simultaneously, the winners playing it out in a final round containing $\sqrt{N}$ winners. There is no advantage in such a wider spreading tree, and in fact it can be shown that a binary tree is optimal. Treesort3 remains the supreme method among the selection sort methods.

1.3 Insertion sorts

These sorting techniques, like the selection techniques, build up the sorted set item at a time, but do so by taking an arbitrary element from the unsorted input set, placing it in the correct position within the elements so far sorted in the output set. The general method is:

ALGORITHM 5.5. *Insertion sort: general method*
1. $k \leftarrow 1$; **while** $k \leq N$ **do**
2. $\quad$ ₁[Choose arbitrary item **x** from input set;

161

3.   Insert x into output set so that output set remains sorted;

4. $k \leftarrow k+1;]_1$

5. **Exit**.

All insertion sorts are, or can be made, stable, so that order of presentation is preserved for items with the same key. In practice the items could be read in one at a time from an external source, so the internal storage of the input set is often unnecessary.

Let us look at a simple example of insertion sorting, using a bubbling technique to make the insertion. The input set is in vector $a[k+1 : N]$ while the output set is in vector $a[1 : k]$. Compare this routine with bubble selection sort Routines 5.2.

ROUTINES 5.6. *Bubble insertion sort*

1. $k \leftarrow 1$; **while** $k < N$ **do**
2. $_1$[choose $a[k+1]$ for insertion ¢
          copy $\leftarrow a[k+1]$;
3.   ¢ bubble insert this into $a[1 : k]$ ¢
          $j \leftarrow k$; **while** $j \geq 1$ **do**
             $_2$[**if** $a[j] <$ copy
                then$[a[j+1] \leftarrow a[j]; j \leftarrow j-1]$
                else$[a[j+1] \leftarrow$ copy; $j \leftarrow -1]$
             $]_2$
          if $j = 0$ **then**$[a[1] \leftarrow$ copy];
4. $k \leftarrow k+1;]_1$
5. **Exit**.

This routine is of the same order of efficiency as bubble selection sort, having of order N^2 comparisons to perform the sort, which is not good enough. Like bubble selection sort, it is a sort-improving method.

Now compare Routines 5.6 with the method used for sorted sequential tables in vector storage, Routines 4.3. There we inserted an item by bubbling it in, and following the discussions there, could improve our bubble insertion sort by placing copy in $a[0]$, and then looping at step 3 under the control of $a[j] >$ copy in the **while** condition, when we must terminate before or at $j = 0$, and have thus saved the tests on j within the loop.

The comparison of bubble insertion sort with the earlier table technique is significant. Indeed, section 4.1 on internal tables provides us with all the basic methods for insertion sorting. The table itself forms the output set, the Insert routine being used at step 3, Algorithm 5.5, with a possible application of the Printout routine to transform the output set into a vector at the end, step 5.

Looking to section 4.1 for efficient methods which are generally applicable, we find two techniques, Comparison Tree tables, and Hash tables. Carrying these ideas across into sorting techniques, we obtain the following routines.

ROUTINES 5.7. *Comparison tree insertion sort*
0. Initialise free area for simple acquisition only of records;
1. $k \leftarrow 1$; **while** $k \leq N$ **do**
2. $_1[\cent$ take next item from input set, $a[k]$ $\cent$
3.   Insert($a[k]$); $\cent$ use insertion routine of Routines 4.8 to insert item $a[k]$ into chained comparison tree table $\cent$
4. $k \leftarrow k+1;]_1$
5. $\cent$ Traverse tree in-order, to obtain sorted set $\cent$
    Printout; $\cent$ as Routines 4.8 $\cent$ **Exit**.

ROUTINES 5.8. *Address calculation sort*
0. Initialise free area if using chaining for resolution of collisions;
1. $k \leftarrow 1$; **while** $k \leq N$ **do**
2. $_1[\cent$ take next item from input set, $a[k]$ $\cent$
3.   Insert($a[k]$); $\cent$ use insertion routine from Routines 4.9 if using rehashing (linear$\pm$1), or from Routines 4.10 if using chaining. The hash and other insertion operations must be order preserving $\cent$
4. $k \leftarrow k+1;]_1$
5. $\cent$ extract the sorted set from the table by using the Printout routine of Routines 4.9 or 4.10 as appropriate $\cent$
    Printout; **Exit**.

Comparison tree insertion sort (called various other names, such as 'monkey puzzle sort') requires two pointers per item, and thus requires an extra $2N$ storage slots for these. There does not need to be a separate input area, for the data can be loaded into the free area at step 0, and then the insertion takes the form of setting the pointer values in the records. A separate output area might be necessary, if

COMPUTATIONAL STRUCTURES

the items are required sorted within a vector of storage. The time taken, as measured by the number of comparisons, is of order $N \log_2 N$, from Hibbard's Theorem, Theorem 4.1. The worst case is of order N^2.

Address calculation sort will involve only of order $2N$ comparisons if we use chained resolution of collisions with a primary table of N pointers, while storage requirements would be for N items, and $2N$ pointers. With rehashing to resolve the collisions in a table of size $2N$ we would require of the order of 1·5 comparisons only. These figures are very impressive, but we must understand just why address calculation sorts appear to work so well. The analysis on which these figures are based, Theorems 4.2 and 4.3, assumed that the data was distributed in a known way, such that after hashing, the hash addresses were uniformly distributed. It is this extra information about the data, the knowledge of its distribution (not the distribution of the actual data values, but the distribution of the parent population from which the data values were drawn), that improves the efficiency from the $N \log_2 N$ figure deduced from information theory, to be of the order of only N comparisons. Where the distribution of the data is not known, and assuming it is uniformly distributed is as much an assumption as any other distribution, address calculation sort could prove disastrous. The worst case occurs when all the items hash to the same position in the table, when the method degenerates to a sequential scan method involving of order N^2 comparisons.

The insertion sorts that we have seen have all had worst cases of order N^2, and so have something of a gamble attached. For small sets of data, the bubble insertion method, Routines 5.8, is adequate, while for medium to large sets of data (more than 20 items) if the distribution is known, use address calculation sort. Comparison tree insertion sort will only exceptionally be justified.

5.1.4 Distribution sorts

These methods are the natural computer-based versions of the manual sorting methods commonly used, for example, in the post office, where the letters are sorted into bins which are then further sorted, and so on.

164

Let us denote the original set to be sorted by A; this has its elements distributed into p subsets $A_1, A_2, ..., A_n$ such that

$$A_1 < A_2 \ ... \ < A_n$$

where $A_k < A_{k+1}$ means that, given an element x of A_k and element y of A_{k+1}, we have $x \leq y$. This then gives:

ALGORITHM 5.9. *Distribution sort, general method*
Distribution sort (A);
1. **if** A is a trivial set, that is, empty or a single element **then[Exit]**
2.   **else**$_1$[Partition A into $A_1, ..., A_n$ with $A_1 < ... < A_p$.
3. $i \leftarrow 1$; **while** $i \leq p$ **do** [Distribution sort(A_i)]]$_1$
4.   **Exit**.

The original mechanical form of this was Radix Sort, still used on mechanical card sorters. The sort key divides into digits, and the data is partitioned using the most significant digit, the sets formed being further partitioned one the second most significant digit, and so on, as illustrated in Fig. 5.7 for digit set {A,B,C}. In fact normal

$\overline{\text{BAB}}$		$\overline{\text{ACC}}$		$\overline{\text{ABC}}$		$\overline{\text{ABB}}$
CAB		ABC		ABB		$\overline{\text{ABC}}$
ACC	1st →	ABB	2nd →	ACC	3rd →	ACC
ABC		$\overline{\text{BAB}}$		$\overline{\text{BAB}}$		BAB
CAA		CAB		CAB		$\overline{\text{CAA}}$
$\overline{\text{ABB}}$		$\overline{\text{CAA}}$		$\overline{\text{CAA}}$		CAB

Fig. 5.7. Example illustrating Radix sort for a digit set A,B,C and keys formed of three digits. The horizontal bars show the divisions between the subsets as the partitioning of the set is successively refined through three cycles of radix partitioning.

mechanical sorting would start at the **least** (rightmost) significant digit, and having distributed, combined, redistribute, and so on working left towards the most significant digit. In this form the radix sort method does not fit into the framework of Algorithm 5.9: nevertheless it is a distribution method, exploiting stability in the radix distribution process.

Radix sort can be used on digital computers, and is in fact **extremely good**. It is best programmed distributing the items using

165

the least significant (rightmost) digit first. Let us sketch the requirements for a radix sort, in Algorithm 5.10. Suppose that we have a
routine Digit(a,j) which finds the jth digit of the key of item a.
Suppose that altogether there are M digits, with digit 1 being the
least significant, digit M being the most significant, and suppose
that digits have radix r, that is, lie between 0 and $r-1$.

ALGORITHM 5.10. *Radix sort*
Indexed set $A = \{a_1, a_2, ..., a_N\}$ initially unsorted.
1. Radix sort(A);
    1.1. $j \leftarrow 1$; **while** $j \leq M$ **do**
    1.2. $_1[i \leftarrow 0$; **while** $i < r$ **do** $[A_i \leftarrow \phi; i \leftarrow i+1;]$
          ¢ the sets $A_0, ..., A_{r-1}$ in the partition are starting empty ¢
    1.3. $k \leftarrow 1$; **while** $k \leq N$ **do**
          $_2[$¢ distribute a_k to appropriate A_i ¢
    1.4.   Take next item a_k from set A;
    1.5. $i \leftarrow$ Digit(a_k,j);
    1.6. $A_i \leftarrow A_i \cup \{a_k\};]_2$
    1.7.   ¢ combine sets A_i to reform A, with indexing of A such
          that all elements of A_i are below those of A_{i+1}, for
          all i. ¢
          $A \leftarrow A_0 \cup A_1 \cup ... \cup A_{r-1};$
        $]_1$
    1.8. **Exit.**
2. Digit(a,j); ¢ accesses the jth digit of the key of item a, where
    $j = 1$ indicates the rightmost, least significant, digit of the key. ¢

The actual sets $A_0, A_1, ..., A_{r-1}$ are best stored using one way chaining. At step 1.4 we just follow a pointer to obtain the next item in
the chained sequence which is set A, while the addition of this item
to the selected set A_i would be done at the **end** of the chained sequence
for set A_i. At the end of each round of radix distributions, at step 1.7,
the sets would have their chains joined end to end, so that the final
null pointer of A_0 is changed to point to A_1, and so on.

Radix sort does not involve comparisons, and so does not fit into
the framework of analysis that we are using. We have M digits,
and thus have M rounds of distributions, each time distributing N
items in steps 1.4, 1.5, and 1.6. Thus we execute steps 1.4, 1.5, and 1.6
MN times. If M is small (and thus r is large), then this is much better

that the $N \log_2 N$ to which we aspire. The comparison between MN and $N \log_2 N$ is especially favourable for large N. Radix sort is not dependent on subtle assumptions about the distribution of the data. But how has radix sort managed to beat our $N \log_2 N$ lower limit? The answer is quite simple. With radix sort we recognise that once items have been encoded within the computer, a lot of the work of sorting has already been done. The act of encoding items into bit patterns effectively involves the comparison of the new item against a set of standards, usually by humans as they key punch the information ready for input to the computer. Why repeat this work?

Radix sort is, of course, suitable for keys composed of strings of symbols. Typically $r = 36$, the alphabet being composed of the letters and numerals, while $M = 8$. For more than 256 items, radix sort becomes preferable. Radix sort can, however, be readily applied to data with numeric keys. For example, for positive integers encoded as binary numbers, we can group the bits together in, say, eights, and think of the number, not as a binary number, but as a number represented to radix $2^8 = 256$. Then if we have set aside 32 bits for the number, we have 4 digits. $M = 4$. On most computers we could very easily obtain each digit separately, and the routine Digit would be trivial.

Hence we conclude, always consider using a radix sort for large quantities of data, and only use another method if the sort key does not decompose readily into a few digits.

However, there are occasions when radix sort is not appropriate. The modern counterpart of radix sort is called Quicksort, and was discovered in 1961 by C. A. R. Hoare.

For Quicksort let us consider the input set A to be stored in the vector $a[m:n]$, and let us split this set into 3 subsets, $a[m:j] < a[j+1:i-1] < a[i:n]$ where the central set consists of a single element, and thus $j+1 = i-1$. The partitioning process itself can vary: in the original algorithm, it chose a 'random' index f between m and n, and then used the value $d = a[f]$ to divide the set. At the end of the partitioning the central set will be the single value d, suitably moved from $a[f]$ to $a[g]$ so that $a[m:g-1]$ are all less than d and $a[g+1:n]$ are all larger than d. By scanning upwards from m and downwards from n pairs of elements that are in the wrong order are located and swapped: and so on until the two scans cross, when all that remains is to shift the value d to the dividing position. For details, see *C.A.C.M.* Algorithm 64 (July 1961).

Quicksort requires extra storage for its essential recursion, of order $\log_2 N$, and by applying Hibbard's Theorem can be shown to have time efficiency of order $N \log_2 N$, with a worst case of N^2.

There have been many variations on this basic algorithms, which have varied in the way they obtain the splitting value, from samples of size k (Sample sort, MacKellar and Frazer) or by delaying the precise choice and using instead an interval which is gradually narrowed (van Emden). The better variations also avoid all but the essential recursion.

Quicksort is the basis for the extraction of order statistics—we see that we can find the median or any other percentile, by partitioning, deciding in which subset the percentile must lie, by considering the sizes of the subsets arising from a partitioning operation, and then further partitioning only the subset appropriate. Recursion is not necessary, and we do not sort the whole set, but only just enough to obtain the percentile desired. See *C.A.C.M.* Algorithm 410 (Chambers), 'partial sorting' (May 1971), pp. 357–8, for further details.

Observe how Selection Sorts are special cases of Distribution Sorts, where the partitioning is arranged so that the original set A is divided into only two subsets, with one subset containing a single element, the smallest (or largest) element, with the other subset containing the remaining elements.

5.1.5 Merge sorts

These sorting methods work on the principle of splitting an unsorted set A into subsets $A_1, A_2, ..., A_p$ in **any** fashion, then sorting $A_1, A_2, ..., A_p$ separately by the same method, then recombining the subsets by merging to form a new permuted A which is sorted. We have seen the basic idea of merging previously but let us look at the special form it takes when merging is used for sorting. Suppose that we have two sets X and Y which are sorted (i.e., $x_i \leq x_j$ if and only if $i < j$), and consider combining them to form a new set Z. For z_1 we choose the smaller of x_1 and y_1, and, supposing x_1 were chosen, we would then for z_2 choose the smaller of x_2 and y_1, and so on. Fig. 5.8 shows a simple example.

Input sets		Item selected	Output set Z
X	Y		
{1,2,6,8}	{3,4,7}	1	empty
{2,6,8}	{3,4,7}	2	{1}
{6,8}	{3,4,7}	3	{1,2}
{6,8}	{4,7}	4	{1,2,3}
{6,8}	{7}	6	{1,2,3,4}
{8}	{7}	7	{1,2,3,4,6}
{8}	empty	8	{1,2,3,4,6,7}
empty	empty	–	{1,2,3,4,6,7,8}

Fig. 5.8. Merging two sorted sets to form a single sorted set.

Let us record this idea as an algorithm. We need three indices, i, j, and k to point to the current position in sets X, Y, and Z respectively, and as we step through X and Y to form Z we must check to see when we reach the end of the sets—and then arrange to copy across the remainder of whichever set was not exhausted to Z. The simple way to do this is to test both i and j separately, but let us here rather use an alternative idea, that we have suggested using but have not used, of putting in dummy end items to mark the end of the set. Thus initially we set x_{n+1} and y_{m+1} to a very large quantity, $+\infty$, and only test k for termination of the merge, thus obtaining the following compact and efficient method.

ALGORITHM 5.11. *Merging sorted sets X and Y to form sorted set Z*
$X = \{x_1, x_2, ..., x_n\}$ and $Y = \{y_1, y_2, ..., y_m\}$.
1. ¢ set terminating items in input sets X and Y ¢
   $x_{n+1} \leftarrow +\infty$; $y_{m+1} \leftarrow +\infty$;
2. ¢ initialise set indices ¢
   $i \leftarrow 1$; $j \leftarrow 1$; $k \leftarrow 1$;
3. **while** $k \leq n+m$ **do**
4.   ₁[¢ transfer smallest input item to output ¢
      if $x_i < y_j$ **then**[$z_k \leftarrow x_i$; $i \leftarrow i+1$;]
                        else[$z_k \leftarrow y_j$; $j \leftarrow j+1$;]
5. $k \leftarrow k+1$;]₁
6. **Exit**.

169

The number of comparisons involved in merging two sets X and Y is just $|X|+|Y| = n+m$. If we use vector storage for the sets X, Y, and Z this means using of order $2N$ storage slots for N items, using pointers to the items if these are bulky, manipulating only the pointers during sorting. We could alternatively use chaining for the sets X, Y, and Z, and simply change pointer values during the merge process, saving storage since the input sets and the output set can share the same storage.

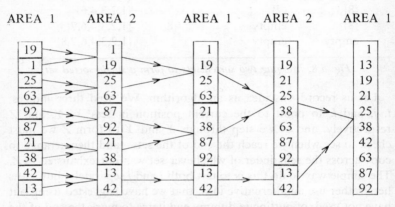

Fig. 5.9. Merge sort of 10 items of data. Arrows show merges, and heavy horizontal lines show divisions between subsets.

The simplest form of merge sort in vector storage starts with subsets consisting of single items, merges these pairwise to form $[N/2]$ sorted subsets each of 2 elements, merge these pairwise again to double the size of the sorted subsets, and halve the number of them, and so on until a single subset, of the sorted data, remains. This is shown in Fig. 5.9, shunting the data back and forth between two areas of storage. Notice how, because the number of items being sorted is not a power of 2, the size of the subsets are not all the same at any given stage of the process. This method of sorting is stable, but is *not* sort-improving because it uses two areas of storage. In each set of merges from one area to the other, there are less than N item comparisons, and altogether there $\log_2 N$ sets of merges, and thus we find that there are of order $N \log_2 N$ comparisons to complete the sorting. We have a method of as good an order of efficiency as we can expect. In fact we can do better than Routines 5.11, because by some clever programming we can exploit any initial ordering in the data. Fig. 5.10 shows the data used in Fig. 5.9, but showing that working from left to right there are five and not 10 sorted subsets! The data is partially sorted already, and this idea has been exploited by Boothroyd in Stringsort, *C.A.C.M.* Algorithm 207 (October 1963), p. 615. In Boothroyd's method, the data is scanned from **both** ends. The method is awkward, and not worth studying further.

Seq.1	Seq.2	Seq.3	Seq.4	Seq.5
19	1, 25, 63, 92	87	21, 38, 42	13

Fig. 5.10. Initial partial sorting of data which can be exploited during merge sorting. Sequence found already sorted when working from left to right.

Now, if we use chained storage for the sets, we do obtain a simple sort method. In an initial phase the data would be formed into a collection of sorted sets, exploiting any natural sorting of the data. These are then merged in pairs, then the resulting sets merged in pairs, and so on until a single sorted set results. During the whole process only the pointers are manipulated, and data is never moved. We could choose to store the collection of sets either as a vector of pointers to the chained sequences, or as a chained sequence of records with two pointer fields, one to the set and one to the next record in the sequence. In either case, the essential steps are given in the following algorithm.

ALGORITHM 5.12. *Chained merge sort*
1. Form up the data into sorted chained sets $A_1,...,A_M$. Store collection either as a vector of pointers, or as a chained sequence of pointers, to these sets.
2. **while** $M > 1$ **do**
3. $_1[k \leftarrow 1$; **while** $k < M$ **do**
4. $_2$[Merge A_k with A_{k+1} to form a new A_j, where $j = \lfloor(k+1)/2\rfloor$;
5. $k \leftarrow k+2$;
    $]_2$

171

6. ¢ if a single set remains unmerged, copy it across ¢
   if $k = M$ **then** copy pointer to A_M so that A_M becomes the new A_m with $m = \lfloor(M+1)/2\rfloor$;
7. $M \leftarrow \lfloor(M+1)/2\rfloor$;
   $]_1$
8. ¢ the single set A_1 that remains is the required set ¢
   Exit.

Finally, let us observe that Insertion Sorts are special cases of Merge Sorts, where at each merge operation we merge two subsets, one of which consists of a single element and is thus trivially sorted, while the other subset is the output set so far formed.

5.1.6 Assessment of internal sorts

We have now seen a variety of internal sorting methods. Good methods involve of the order of $N \log_2 N$ comparisons to sort the data, while simple methods involve of the order of N^2 comparisons. Two methods, Address Calculation sort and Radix sort, use extra information about the data and reduce the number of 'comparisons' required to the order of N. Ideally the sorting methods should use no extra storage over and above that required for the data items, and a fixed amount of storage for the algorithms and its control. Many methods use extra storage, of the order of $\log_2 N$ or N. In choosing a method for sorting we must take into account the trade-off between time and space and programming effort. We must also take into account the form of the data, and whether we should sort pointers to the data rather than the data itself (see section 4.1.4 for a discussion of data and pointer sizes). We conclude that the best choices of internal sorting methods will usually be:

(i) For ease of programming: bubble insertion sort using a dummy end record to control the scan (see Exercise 1, section 5.3).
(ii) When N is large, efficiency is important, and the key can be decomposed into a small number of digits: radix sort, Algorithm 5.10.
(iii) When efficiency is important and space is at a premium; Treesort3, Routines 5.4.

(iv) When the distribution of the population from which that data is drawn is known, extra storage is available, and the N^2 worst case can be tolerated; address calculations sort, Routines 5.8.

.2 External sorts

Now suppose that we have a very large file, much too large to fit into the random access core storage of the computer. It is thus quite impossible to sort the file using an internal sorting method, so we must sort the file in stages.

All methods which sort a file externally use internal sorts to the maximum extent possible, and thereafter use a file merge strategy. The overall strategy is to read into the computer as many records as will fit, sort these internally, then output them as a sorted block or sequence, and repeat this until all the file has been formed into blocks, each of which is sorted. Then in a second phase we merge the blocks two (or more) at a time, so reducing the number of blocks and increasing their size until we are left with a single block, the file completely sorted.

Let us look at a simple example, so as to obtain a feel for what is involved. Suppose that we have 1,700 records of data, stored on a magnetic tape. Each record consists of 300 characters of information, and our computer storage is limited to 32,000 characters storage. Hence we can only fit approximately 100 records into the computer at one time for internal sorting. (It is approximately 100, since the programs require storing.) Suppose that we also have four magnetic tape drives which we can use for sorting our file. Then one method for sorting the file is shown within Fig. 5.11. We start by having the unsorted file on a single tape, on drive T_4, and read in 100 records, sort these with one of the methods of the last section, and output to a tape on drive T_1, input the next 100 records from the file, sort these internally, and output to the tape on drive T_2, then sort the next 100 records, outputting to T_1, and so on alternatively outputting sorted blocks of 100 records to T_1 then T_2. We end up with 9 blocks of 100 records on T_1 and 8 blocks of 100 records on T_2, denoting these as 9(100) and 8(100) respectively. We rewind the tapes ready for the second phase of our sorting. We input the records at the start of T_1 and T_2 (one record from each), compare their keys,

173

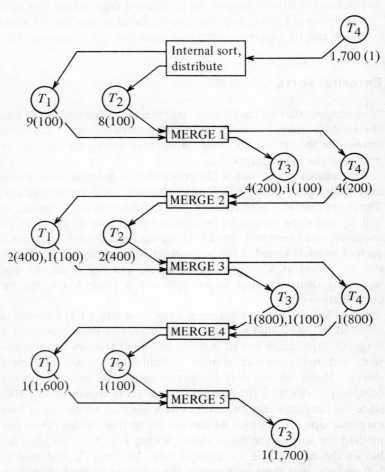

Fig. 5.11. Sorting 1,700 records using four tape-decks in a balanced two-way merge. Circles indicate tapes, and arrows show the direction of flow of the records. The tapes are numbered to show which tape-deck is intended, and below each circle is an indication of number and size of the sorted blocks. (p) indicates a block of p records, sorted, while n(p) indicates n such blocks following one another on the tape, and n(p), m(q) indicates that on the tape there are first of all n blocks each of p records, followed by m blocks each of q records.

$$M = 1{,}700, \; n = 100, \; N = 17.$$

and output the smaller to T_3, and input a new record from T_1 or T_2 as appropriate to replace the record output. Thus we continue, merging the first block of T_1 with the first block of T_2, until both these first blocks have been exhausted, and we have on T_3 one block of 200 records, sorted. On T_1 we now have 8 blocks of 100 records left, and on T_2 only 7 blocks of 100 records. We merge the next block on T_1 with the next block on T_2, outputting this time to T_4. So we merge a block from T_1 with a block from T_2, alternatively outputting to T_3 and T_4, until T_2 is empty, T_1 has a single block of 100 records left on it, and each of T_3 and T_4 have four blocks of 200 records on them. We end this cycle by copying the final block across from T_1 to T_3, thus ending up with four blocks of 200 records followed by one block of 100 records, on T_3, and four blocks of 200 records on T_4. A similar cycle of merging from T_3 and T_4 alternatively to T_1 and T_2 leads to two blocks each of 400 records followed by one of 100 records, on T_1, and two blocks each of 400 records on T_2. Another three cycles of merging then lead to all the data sorted on T_3, as shown in Fig. 5.11.

The preceding example serves to bring out several important points. There are two distinct phases during the sorting, a phase where the computer is used to its capacity internally sorting records into as large blocks as possible, distributing them to two or more tapes: the exact form of the distribution depends upon the particular merging process that follows. Then in a second phase, blocks of records are merged into larger and larger blocks, through several cycles, until eventually all the data is contained in a single sorted block. The merge phase only requires a small amount of computer storage, since merging from k tapes only requires that there are k records internal at any one time. In our example, $k = 2$. On the other hand, we do tie up the tape drives for the duration of the sorting process.

Suppose that we start with M records which require sorting, and that the capacity of our computer is such that only n records can be sorted internally, with $n \ll M$. This means that during the internal sorting phase, we shall form $\left\lceil \dfrac{M}{n} \right\rceil = N$ blocks which then require merging to eventually form a single sorted block. However, as we shall see in the next section, we can do better than this using the 'replacement principle'.

We are concerned with the total time taken by the sorting process, primarily as a function of M, the number of records to be sorted. The internal sort and distribution phase involves inputting n records, and internally sorting them. The form of internal sort to choose is a selection method, using replacement (see the next section). This permits the concurrent input of a record, the selection of a record for output, and the output of a record, if suitably programmed. Unless the records are very small (and hence n the size of the internal sort is large) this phase will be dominated by input/output time rather than selection time, especially if an efficient selection method has been used. The second merge phase is completely input/output dominated. The whole sorting process is thus completely dominated by the time taken to input and output records, and the total time taken to sort the file will be proportional to the total number of records passed through the computer during the sort process. We shall call this the **volume passed** V, and use this as the index of performance for external sorts. Note that during the merge phase the backing store will be fully utilised, but that the central processor will be almost idle, giving the opportunity for multi-programming if this is possible on the computer.

One important method for sorting magnetic tapes does not in fact divide the sorting process into distinct phases with internal sorting preceding merging: internal sorts and merges occur throughout the sort process, as we will see.

All the external sorting methods that we shall study in detail are designed for sequential files, for magnetic tape files. An important aspect of magnetic tapes is whether or not they can read data backwards. If data can only be read forwards, then the magnetic tapes must be rewound after writing before the data can be read for a next cycle of merges. It is important to exploit backwards reading of magnetic tapes if this is possible, so as to avoid rewinding the magnetic tapes. We shall comment on this possibility where appropriate.

Special sorting methods for other external storage media such as discs and drums will not be covered: the methods given here will provide essential background for the more specialised methods: for further reading, you should read either the book by Knuth (vol. iii) or the book by Flores.

2.1 Replacement internal sorts

With selection sorts, we saw that the basic step was to select the smallest (or largest) item in the input set, and then remove this from the input set, placing it in the output set or outputting directly to an external medium. If the internal sort is part of an external sort, then the latter would happen, the item be output, leaving a space into which a new item could be placed. This new item would be read from the file to be sorted, and then another selection process would be undertaken. Providing that the new item is greater than the one it replaces, all is well, and the sequence output would continue in ascending order. Replacement and selection can then continue until an item is input which is less than the one just output: at this point the new item must be set aside, stored for later use, the set from which the selections are made reduced by one, and then the replacement and selection process repeated. This continues until the selection set has been reduced to nothing, when all the items set aside during the cycle are used to start a new complete cycle of replacement and selection operations. This is set out in more detail below.

ALGORITHM 5.13. *General replacement selection sort*
There are two input sets, $\{a_1,...,a_k\}$ from which the selections are made, and $\{a_{k+1},...,a_n\}$ where the items are stored ready for the next round of selections.
1.   Read in n items to $\{a_1,...,a_n\}$.
     Select an initial output file;
     ¢ set count q for final replacement selection cycle ¢
     $q \leftarrow 0$;
2.   **while** input file not empty **do**
3. $_1$[¢ perform one complete replacement and selection cycle ¢
     $k \leftarrow n$; Initialise selection process in $\{a_1,...,a_n\}$;
     while $k \geq 1$ **do**
4. $_2$[Select smallest item in $\{a_1,...,a_k\}$, say a_j;
5.   Output a_j to current output file;
6.   **if** input file not empty **then**[input next item to b]
                    else[$b \leftarrow -\infty$; $q \leftarrow q+1$]
7.   **while** $b \geq a_j$ **do**
8. $_3$[¢ replace ¢ $a_j \leftarrow b$;
9.   Select smallest item in $\{a_1,...,a_k\}$, say a_j

177

10.   Output a_j to current output file;

11.   **if** input file not empty **then**[input next item to b]
$$\text{else}[b \leftarrow -\infty; q \leftarrow q+1]$$
      $]_3$

12.   ¢ set aside b for next cycle, reduce selection set ¢
$$a_j \leftarrow a_k; a_k \leftarrow b; k \leftarrow k-1;$$
      $]_2$

13.   Mark end of ascending output sequence (say with a dummy item of $+\infty$);

Change current output file as appropriate for External Sort method;
    $]_1$

14.   ¢ on final round q items of $-\infty$ were placed in $\{a_1,...,a_q\}$ ¢
Internally sort and output $\{a_{q+1},...,a_n\}$.

15.   **Exit.**

In implementing Algorithm 5.13 we would store the sets as vectors of records, and may very likely sort pointers to the records, rather than the records themselves. Selection of the smallest at steps 4 and 9 and implicitly at step 14, could be made by the simple method of Routines 5.2, or for efficiency by the Treseort3 method, Routines 5.4, which requires the initialisation in step 3. The end of blocks or ascending sequences of output records could be left implicit at step 13, the end being marked by a change in order, or could be made explicit either with a special record, or a field within a record. The changes in the current output file at step 13 depend upon the particular external sort method into which the replacement selection sort has been inserted, and will be detailed within the methods as they are examined.

Clearly replacement selection sorting must increase the length of the ascending sequences that are output, but by how much? In fact on the average it doubles the lengths of the sequences, so that if n is the length obtained without replacement, then on the average the blocks are of length $2n$, and instead of $N = \left\lceil \dfrac{M}{n} \right\rceil$ blocks, there are now only $N = \left\lceil \dfrac{M}{2n} \right\rceil$ blocks. This reduces the total amount of merging required to complete the external sort, and thus reduces the total time spent in sorting a file. The total work involved during the internal sort phase is not changed, since we still have M selections to make, each involving either n or $\log_2 n$ comparisons, depending upon the selection method.

2.2 Balanced multi-way merge

We have already seen this simplest of methods for externally sorting sequential files, in Fig. 5.11. There we used four magnetic tapes, or sequential files. Let us now generalise this method to an arbitrary number of files.

We shall suppose that we have an even number of tape drives or files, $F_1, F_2, ..., F_{2k}$. Initially the unsorted data is in file F_{2k}, containing M records in all.

In the first phase of the sort the M records on file F_{2k} are read into the computer n at a time and internally sorted, and output to one F_1 to F_k. If we are using a non-replacing sort, then n is constant and as large as the internal storage capacity of the computer will allow, while if we are using a replacement selection sort, n is variable with an average of twice the internal storage capacity. The internal sort is repeated until all of the records have been read from F_{2k} and distributed evenly to $F_1, ..., F_k$. If there are N blocks produced by the internal sorting, then $F_1, ..., F_j$ each contain $\left\lceil \dfrac{N}{k} \right\rceil$ blocks, while the remaining $F_{j+1}, ..., F_f$ each contain 1 block less, $\left\lfloor \dfrac{N}{k} \right\rfloor$ blocks.

In the second phase of the sort, the blocks are merged k at a time, one from each file $F_1, ..., F_k$ with the resulting blocks of kn records being output to $F_{k+1}, ..., F_{2k}$, so that the new blocks are evenly distributed among the k files, there being roughly N/k^2 blocks in each file. A further merge from $F_{k+1}, ..., F_{2k}$ to $F_1, ..., F_k$ then further increases the block size k-fold, and reduces the number of blocks k times. So this continues for $\lceil \log_k N \rceil$ cycles of merging until all the records are in ascending order within a single file.

ALGORITHM 5.14. *Balanced k-way merge*
Altogether we have $K = 2k$ files, with the data starting in file F_{2k}. We use a replacement sort in the initial distribution and internal sort

phase, and later on in merging assume that we can detect empty files, can tell when all the data is in a single file, and can merge when some of the files are empty. A suitable mechanism for performing these actions is to keep a counter for each file recording the total number of blocks left on the file. The values i, p, and q are used for controlling the switch-over from file to file, set of files to set of files.

1. Place data to be sorted in file F_{2k};
    $¢$ Phase 1: internal sort and distribution $¢$
2. $i \leftarrow 0$;
3. Initialise replacement sort (Algorithm 5.13, step 1);
4. **while** F_{2k} not empty **do**
5. $_1[$ $¢$ Algorithm 5.13 $¢$
    Replacement sort from F_{2k} to F_{i+1} until sequence ends;
6. $¢$ change output files, step 13 of Algorithm 5.13 $¢$
    $i \leftarrow i+1$ Modulo k;
    $]_1$
7. Reset (rewind) $F_1,...,F_k$ and F_{2k}.
    $¢$ Phase 2: merge $¢$
8. $p \leftarrow 1$; $q \leftarrow k+1$;
9. **while** data in more than one file of $F_p,...,F_{p+k-1}$ **do**
10. $_2[i \leftarrow 0$;
    while all of $F_p,...,F_{p+k-1}$ not empty **do**
11. $_3[$Merge from $F_p,...,F_{p+k-1}$ to F_{q+i} (Algorithm 5.11);
12. $¢$ change output file $¢$ $i \leftarrow i+1$ Modulo k;
    $]_3$
13. Reset (rewind) all files;
14. Swap values of p and q to swap input and output file sets;
    $]_2$
15. Report that data on file F_p.
16. **Exit**.

In the algorithm, the replacement sort has been built into phase 1, though the details have been skipped over, and can be extracted readily from Algorithm 5.13. For the k-way merges at step 11, a generalisation of Algorithm 5.11 is required: this has been left as an exercise, number 5, section 5.3.

In a multi-way merge backwards reading from magnetic tapes can be readily exploited. In the form presented we have to rewind the magnetic tapes at the end of phase 1, and during phase 2, at steps 7 and 13. However, if we can read backwards, then we can merge the blocks equally well, excepting that the order (ascending or descending) of the blocks reverses when we write them forwards and read them backwards. Reading backwards for the first cycle of merges, we read the blocks in ascending order, and thus write them in ascending order, and so on. Thus on files F_{k+1} to F_{2k} the blocks are always in ascending order, while on files F_1 to F_k they are always in descending order. This only requires small modifications to Algorithm 5.14, and saves all the time spent rewinding the tapes. At the end we may need to copy the final file to reverse the order.

At each cycle of the merge phase, every record passes through the computer, and thus the volume passed per merge cycle is M records. There are $\lceil \log_k N \rceil$ merge cycles, and the internal sort phase, and hence the volume passed is

$$V = M(\lceil \log_k N \rceil + 1) \quad \text{where} \quad N = \left\lceil \frac{M}{2n} \right\rceil,$$

n = capacity in records of internal store.

This is assuming a replacement internal sort. In the example worked through in Fig. 5.11, $M = 1,700$, $n = 100$, a replacement sort was not used, so $N = 17$, $k = 2$, $\lceil \log_2 N \rceil = 5$, and thus $V = 10,200$.

This multi-way merge method of sorting is very easy to program, and is widely used. It requires a minimum of four tape-decks, though the more tape-decks that are available, the faster will be the sort. An odd number of files or tape-decks can be exploited, see Exercise 8, section 5.3.

.3 Polyphase merge

If we have K files to work with, then in principle we should be able to merge from $K-1$ of the files to the remaining file, and thus exploit as wide a merge as possible. In balanced multi-way merging we were only merging from half the files, and just under half the files were idle at any one time. How can we make fuller use of our resources, merge from $K-1$ files at all times?

Arranging to merge from as many files as possible turns out to be quite a complex operation. We must distribute our sorted blocks formed during the internal sort and distribute phase *unevenly* among

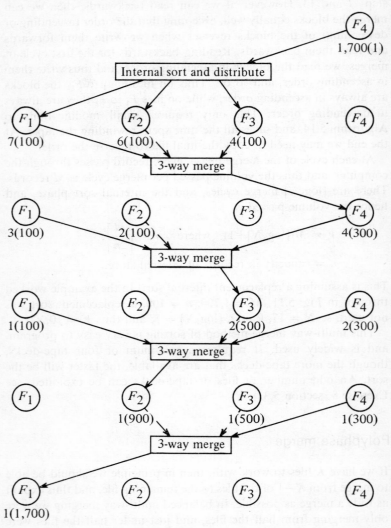

Fig. 5.12. Example illustrating a Polyphase Merge Sort. There are four work files, with the unsorted data initially in F_4. We start with 1,700 records in F_4, and internally sort 100 records at a time. Thus $M = 1,700$ and $n = 100$. The number of blocks per file, p, and the size of the blocks q, is indicated as $p(q)$, as in Fig. 5.11.

the files, before merging so that only one file ever becomes empty at one moment, apart from the final merge. The original method was called Cascade Merge, but this has been completely superseded by Polyphase Merge which is always better. Let us examine an example.

As in the 2-way merge example (Fig. 5.11), let us consider $M = 1,700$ records, use an internal sort without replacement with $n = 100$, and use 4 work files or tape-decks. A Polyphase merge sort of the file leads to the diagram of Fig. 5.12. During the internal sort phase we distribute the 17 blocks unevenly, with 7 blocks in F_1, 6 in F_2 and 4 in F_3. We then merge from F_1, F_2, and F_3 to F_4, until F_3 is empty. This leaves us with 3 blocks in F_1, 2 in F_2, and 4 blocks each of 300 records in F_4. Now merge from F_1, F_2, and F_4 to F_3 until F_2 is empty, and so on, as in Fig. 5.12. We end up with all the data in F_1, having at all stages used 3-way merges. During internal sorting all 1,700 records passed through the computer, and during merges, successively 1,200, 1,000, 900, and finally 1,700 records passed, giving a total volume passed of 6,500 records. Contrast this with the 10,200 records passed for 2-way balanced merging! This example is somewhat unfair, since it is a perfect example for Polyphase Merge, and a worst possible example for Balanced, but the figures are indicative of potential savings.

If we try any other distribution of the 17 blocks formed by the internal sort and distribution phase, we fail, for the merges do not continue as 3-way merges to the end. For example, 6(100), 6(100), 5(100) after the first merge cycle gives 1(100), 1(100), 5(300) and after the second merge empties two tapes and we are then stuck with a 2-way merge. How can we know the correct distribution in order to avoid disasters?

In Fig. 5.12 the number of blocks in the file with the most blocks at the start of any merge cycle, follows the sequence 7 (F_1), 4 (F_4), 2 (F_3), 1 (F_2), 1 (F_1). In the other order this is {1,1,2,4,7}, and these numbers are part of the sequence {0,0,1,1,2,4,7,13,24,50,...} which is a 3rd-order generalised Fibonacci Series. The kth-order Generalised Fibonacci Series is a series of numbers where any element of the series is the sum of the preceding k numbers, defined as

$$_k f_j = 0 \quad \text{for} \quad 0 \le j \le k-2, \quad _k f_{k-1} = 1$$

$$_k f_j = \sum_{i=1}^{k} {}_k f_{j-i}.$$

183

For Polyphase Merges with K files, using $K-1 = k$ way merges, the number of blocks in the fullest file follows a kth order Fibonacci Series. This is fairly easy to prove.

Polyphase is better than balanced for small numbers of tapes, but it is considerably more complex. We will not consider it further, though I recommend further reading of either Flores or Knuth. For large numbers of tapes there is a third method, Oscillating Sort, which exploits backwards read (indeed, they are essential). It is always more efficient than Balanced merges, and so should be considered for external sorting routines that will be used often.

5.3 Exercises

5.3.1 Modify the bubble insertion sort Routines 5.6 to use a dummy terminating record $a[0]$ and thus save on control comparisons. Compare the original routines with your modification of it, experimentally, using the timing methods discussed in Exercise 4.4.4.

5.3.2 Modify the Quicksort Routine (*Communications A.C.M.* (July 1961), Algorithm 64) so that

(*a*) Only the essential recursion remains.

(*b*) Recursion is not used, but a stack is employed to retain the essential values for backtracking.

(*c*) Partitioning is done by van Emden's method using an interval to guide the partitioning: $[d_1, d_2]$ guides the partitioning, starting at $[-\infty, +\infty]$, the interval narrowing each time an element is found within the interval. (Reference: van Emden, *Communications A.C.M.*, vol. 13 (1970), pp. 563–7.)

Compare the various versions of the Quicksort routine for efficiency, using the methods of Exercise 4.4.4.

5.3.3 Look-up Shellsort in the Communications of the A.C.M. (Algorithm 201, August 1963, p. 445). Experiment 'manually' with the algorithm using a small problem (say with 7 numbers, and with 8 numbers) and various values of m. For some values of m the algorithm behaves in a very similar manner to a merge-sort. Would you expect it to be as efficient? Why not? Program the algorithm and compare its efficiency with a bubble sort (Routine 5.2 or 5.6) and with Treesort3 (Routines 5.4).

.4 In the versions of Merge sort that exploit initial partial sorting of the data, roughly what improvement would you expect?

.5 Generalise the merge Algorithm 5.11 to k input sets. Arrange that the selection process for the next element to output takes the form of a tree, in the fashion of Treesort3, Routines 5.4.

.6 Write a general program which will generate a kth order Fibonacci series to the Nth term in the series. Do not store the complete series, only the previous k values necessary for the generation, without shifting these values from one step in the generation to the next.

Add to this program the capability to generate the ideal distribution of blocks among the k-files in preparation for k-way $k+1$ file Polyphase merge.

.7 Implement the method for partial sorting to find order statistics.

.8 Generalise the balanced multi-way merge Routines 5.14 to allow for both an odd number and an even number of work files for use during the sort. Choose the optimal division of the odd number of files.

.9 Write a detailed algorithm for Oscillating Sort.

10 Program all the major internal sort methods presented in this chapter, and compare them experimentally when sorting integers, using the timing techniques of Exercise 4.4.4.

5.3.11 Program the two external sort methods that have been studied in this chapter, using an internal sort without replacement, and using an internal sort with replacement. Investigate their relative efficiencies in terms of volume passed as a function of M the number of records to be sorted, K the number of work files being used, and n the capacity of internal fast access memory. There is no need to use any timing techniques: simply count the number of input and output operations, taking the average over several trials for the replacement sort case. Do not use real external files for your tests, simulate the external files using vectors within a suitable Input/Output routine.

5.3.12 Program a replacement selection Treesort3, storing the binary tree by the alternative vector method as used in logsearch, Fig. 4.8. The binary tree stored in vector $a[i:j]$ has root at $a[[(i+j)/2]]$ with left-subtree in $a[i:[(i+j)/2]-1]$ and right-subtree in $a[[(i+j)/2]+1:j]$. Store **pointers** to the primary data within the tree, setting the pointers to point to a dummy record with an extreme value as the tree size is reduced.

Bibliography

The following books and papers are intended to provide starting points for further study, to take the student of this book more deeply into the many topics that were only just touched on here. Reference to these books and papers was made during the appropriate sections of this book.

Barron, D. W., *Assemblers and Loaders*, 2nd edition (Macdonald/ American Elsevier, 1969).

Bellman, Richard E., *Dynamic Programming* (Princeton University Press/Oxford University Press, 1957).

Berztiss, A. T., *Data Structures, Theory and Practice* (Academic Press, 1971).

Dahl, O.-J., Dijkstra, E. W., and Hoare, C. A. R., *Structured Programming* (Academic Press, 1972).

Date, C. J., *An Introduction to Data Base Systems* (Addison-Wesley, 1975).

Engles, R. W., 'A tutorial on data-base organisation', *Annual Review Automatic Programming*, vol. 7, part 1, pp. 1–65 (Pergamon, 1972).

Flores, Ivan, *Computer Sorting* (Prentice-Hall, 1969).

Foster, J. M., *List Processing* (Macdonald/American Elsevier, 1967).

Gries, David, *Compiler Construction for Digital Computers* (Wiley International Edition, 1971).

Harary, Frank, *Graph Theory* (Addison-Wesley, 1971).

Henley, J. P., *Computer-Based Library and Information Systems*, 2nd edition (Macdonald/American Elsevier, 1970).

Higman, Bryan, *A Comparative Study of Programming Languages* (Macdonald/American Elsevier, 1967).

Hopcroft, John E., and Ullman, Jeffrey D., *Formal Languages and their Relation to Automata* (Addison-Wesley, 1969).

Hopgood, F. R. A., *Compiling Techniques* (Macdonald/American Elsevier, 1969).

Humby, E., *Programs from Decision Tables* (Macdonald/American Elsevier, 1973).

Knuth, Donald E., *The Art of Computer Programming*, vol. 1, *Fundamental Algorithms* (Addison-Wesley, 1968); vol. 2,

Semi-Numerical Algorithms (1969); vol. 3, *Searching and Sorting* (1973).

Lefkovitz, David, *File Structures for On-Line Systems* (Spartan/Macmillan Press, 1969).

Martin, James, *Design of Real-Time Computer Systems* (Prentice-Hall, 1967).

Nilsson, Nils J., *Problem-Solving Methods in Artificial Intelligence* (McGraw-Hill, 1971).

Salton, Gerard, *Automatic Information Organisation and Retrieval* (McGraw-Hill, 1968).

Sammet, Jean A., 'Survey of formula manipulation', *Communications of the A.C.M.*, vol. 9, no. 8 (August 1966), pp. 555–69.

Index

Numbers in **bold** type indicate principal references.